Praise for *In Defense of Dabbling*

"Karen Walrond's *In Defense of Dabbling* is a welcome permission slip to feed our curiosity, to play with and explore whatever it is we're drawn to—not for our side hustle, not to become a professional, but for our humanity. Walrond is the perfect leader for what is sure to be a movement of celebrating all things amateur. Her humility, vulnerability, and earned confidence have motivated me to pick up my favorite long-dormant textile design app!"

—**Gabrielle Blair**, *New York Times* bestselling author, designer, and mother of six

"The wise and delightful Karen Walrond once again guides us straight to the hidden joys and unexpected truths of life. For all of us hoping to make the very best of our time on this earth, she's an essential voice."

—**Katherine Center**, *New York Times* bestselling author

"As someone who has always known that midlife isn't a crisis but a chrysalis, I deeply believe that aging is the same as growing—and that growing is all about continual learning and adventure. *In Defense of Dabbling* provides a blueprint for us to grow: Its 'Seven Attributes of Intentional Amateurism' provide guideposts along our way. This book reminds us of the power we all hold to make our lives bigger, brighter, and more expansive than ever."

—**Chip Conley**, *New York Times* bestselling author

"A life-expanding ode to the joy of being an amateur in a world that's bent on mastery, *In Defense of Dabbling* reminds us to say yes to moments, activities, and pursuits for no other reason than the feelings they give us. A powerful reset, bundled with an invitation to take yourself, and the world, a little more lightly."

—**Jonathan Fields**, award-winning author of *Sparked: Discover Your Unique Imprint for Work That Makes You Come Alive*

"Karen Walrond's voice is unmistakably wise, humane, and joyous. What if our path out of the spiraling psychological crises of our time was as simple as picking up a hobby or two? It's a counterintuitively profound prescription: we need more love, more freedom, more curiosity in our lives. So let's choose it. Not to feed social media or hustle some extra income, but because it's what our soul most needs: room to roam."

—**Sean Fitzpatrick**, psychotherapist, executive director of The Jung Center, and author of *The Ethical Imagination*

"A joyful exploration of play that helped reignite my own creative passions. Like having a long, healing lunch with your best friend."

—**Jenny Lawson**, #1 *New York Times* bestselling author

"I think Karen Walrond might be a little bit of a good witch. It's the only thing that can explain how she always seems to write the exact right book I need at the exact right moment

I need it! This book is a love letter to all of us amateurs who have our own 'abridged list of amateur pursuits' of 'things I tried and didn't try—but still might.' This book is for the dabblers, the fuzzy stargazers, and the intentional amateurs with a great many loves."

—**Marcie Alvis Walker**, author of *Everybody Come Alive*

"Karen Walrond brings us back to the simple joy of doing things just because we want to—no pressure to get it exactly right. She invites us to follow our curiosity, play a little more, and remember what it's like to explore for the fun of it."

—**Meredith Walker**, co-founder of Amy Poehler's Smart Girls

IN DEFENSE OF DABBLING

IN DEFENSE OF DABBLING

THE BRILLIANCE OF BEING A TOTAL AMATEUR

KAREN WALROND

Broadleaf Books
Minneapolis

IN DEFENSE OF DABBLING
The Brilliance of Being a Total Amateur

31 30 29 28 27 26 25 1 2 3 4 5 6 7 8 9

Library of Congress Cataloging-in-Publication Data

Names: Walrond, Karen, author.
Title: In defense of dabbling : the brilliance of being a total amateur / Karen Walrond.
Description: Minneapolis : Broadleaf Books, [2025]
Identifiers: LCCN 2024061761 (print) | LCCN 2024061762 (ebook) | ISBN 9781506487656 (hardback) | ISBN 9781506487663 (ebook)
Subjects: LCSH: Amateurism.
Classification: LCC GV14.45 .W35 2025 (print) | LCC GV14.45 (ebook) | DDC 790.1--dc23/eng/20250203
LC record available at https://lccn.loc.gov/2024061761
LC ebook record available at https://lccn.loc.gov/2024061762

Cover design by Amanda Kain
Cover image: © 2025 Getty Images; Watercolor Textured Background/ 887755698 by ivanastar

Print ISBN: 978-1-5064-8765-6
eBook ISBN: 978-1-5064-8766-3

Printed in India.

Dedicated to Marcus,

my most favorite dabbler

CONTENTS

jack of all trades is a master of none, but oftentimes better than a master of one.

-unknown

1

A Case for Intentional Amateurism

I AM NOT an expert at anything.

I mean, I do a few things *decently*. In a former life I was a good lawyer, but let's be honest: I was never in danger of being appointed to the Supreme Court. I'm an adequate photographer, but certainly not a great one. I can make a proper meal, but I'm no chef. I even Hula-Hoop, but I can't do one single trick.

While washing up the dishes after dinner one evening, I made this observation to my partner, Marcus. "That is patently untrue," he responded, as he leaned against the pantry door. "You're good at a lot of things."

"Am I?" I countered. I shut off the faucet and turned to look at him. "Name one area I'm an expert in."

I waited.

He stared back, silent.

Finally, he spoke. "Well," he said, "does it matter?"

Now it was my turn to be silent. *Did* it matter? Isn't this what we're all supposed to do: make our marks on the world in distinguished ways? Shouldn't I, at my big age, have mastered something noteworthy by now?

Yet Marcus's question stopped me short. While I might not be winning a Nobel Prize anytime soon, my life's not *nothing*. In fact, there's no denying that I'm otherwise content. I'm educated, I've consistently worked, I've traveled. I enjoy being married to a lovely, decent man, and together we've raised a funny, charming, smart young woman. Life has been, dare I say, *good*.

But very little of my good life has anything to do with expertise or mastery. The joy I've had in almost everything I've ever done—from my professional life to parenting—has arisen mostly in the *attempt*.

I'm happy, I thought, *but I might be a total amateur*.

And isn't being an amateur just plain *wrong*?

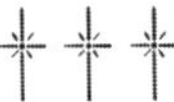

Weeks after that kitchen conversation, I was still ruminating on the true meaning of being an amateur. On one hand, the word *amateur* is often used as a stand-in for "incompetent," or "unskillful," or even "shoddy." Think about it: Would you ever consider buying a car that featured "amateur workmanship"? Or how would you feel if you made a mistake at work and your boss described it as an "amateur move"? Being associated with the word "amateur" is the last thing any of us want. And yet, the expectation of being an expert in everything we do is *exhausting*. Besides, my life hadn't seemed to suffer for my amateurism. I even suspected that it was *because* I'm an amateur that I was content. So why was I so conflicted?

The attorney in me can't help but get to the bottom of a paradox, so I looked up the word *amateur* to see if it has always been used as a pejorative. To my surprise, it hasn't. According to the *Oxford English Dictionary*, the word *amateur* is derived from the Latin *amare*, meaning "to love," and *amator*, meaning "lover." The French furthered the word's evolution into *amateur*, which, at the time, meant "a lover of art and, by implication, often a collector." By the eighteenth century, the word's English connotation had transformed again, now referencing "someone who practiced art for pleasure and interest, but not for money." By all accounts, it appeared that, historically speaking, the amateur was all about love, appreciation, and passion.

I'm liking this, I thought.

But then I kept reading.

Things went south around the turn of the nineteenth century, when use of the term *amateur* became less kind. According to *Merriam-Webster*, by 1790, the word was already being used in the somewhat condescending extended sense: British House of Commons member George Rous snidely described his colleague, Edmund Burke, as "a bystander, a mere amateur of aristocracy" in his *Thoughts on Government.* Several not-so-nice synonyms have since popped up: *dilettante*, for example, and *neophyte*. These terms imply that embarking on any task of avocation isn't worth it unless we're doing so with the intent of mastery. Nowadays, the only positive meanings of "amateur" are either used in sports (to distinguish one athlete from another who chooses to go “pro”) or as a strategy toward mastery (an “amateur mindset” as a step toward becoming more proficient, more successful, more perfect).

Despite everything I was reading, I couldn’t find any calls to reclaim the word in its original fullness: the amateur as one who finds pleasure in an activity, who collects art or beauty, or who practices something because they’re interested in it, rather than to make money. As far as I could tell, no one was making the case for using the word to mean a person who loves pursuing an avocation, simply because *they love pursuing the avocation.* And nowhere was it suggested that seeking to be an amateur as an end goal, in and of itself, is a worthy pursuit.

Honestly, I blame “hustle culture”: the societal expectation to be productive at all costs. From social media to self-help books, the advice is ubiquitous: The acquisition of money, power, and mastery is the only way to live a successful life. Unsurprisingly, this has deleterious effects. Rainesford Stauffer, a young journalist and the author of the book *An Ordinary Age: Finding Your Way in a World That Expects Exceptional*, laments that “striving to be extraordinary, being exceptional, and being special are the same as being capable, being fulfilled, and being happy.” This pressure makes it almost impossible to do things simply for enjoyment’s sake. “Sometimes, the deeper we get into adulthood, the more ‘free time’ pursuits get crossed off the list,” she writes. “There’s a cost to having hobbies, and if an activity happens to be free, it demands some freedom of time that a lot of young adults simply don’t have.” This sentiment is echoed by others: A friend of mine described a conversation she had about this very topic with a coworker. "As a young Black woman, I feel a lot of pressure to excel in my career—to honor my family, as well as my culture," her colleague reflected. "And I think sometimes I'm so focused on doing that, I've forgotten how to be interesting."

I have to say, this broke my heart a little.

But the echo kept repeating: Another friend, who is undeniably accomplished in her work, admits that she has a habit of always moving on to the next thing without taking any downtime, even to appreciate what she's already accomplished. An acquaintance told me that when she does find time to do something creative outside of her job, societal pressures impel her to turn it into a "side hustle"—thus, in effect, landing her with *two* jobs she's required to excel at. Still another laments, "It kills me, because I never feel like I'm doing enough, and I'm exhausted. I can't keep the pace of other creators or makers or even teachers." Almost every time I asked people how hustle culture affects their lives, they repeated "I'm exhausted," or "I'm never enough." The societal pressure is real, and it is *crushing*.

As if that's not enough, all this hustling can lead to perfectionism, which is a whole other concentric circle of hell. My friend Brené Brown, a pioneering researcher on shame, courage, and vulnerability, is emphatic when she distinguishes perfectionism from healthy striving: "Perfectionism is the belief that if we live perfect, look perfect, and act perfect, we can minimize or avoid the pain of blame, judgment, and shame," she writes. Dr. Tracy Dennis-Tiwary, a psychology and neuroscience professor, goes even further: "The relentless pursuit of flawlessness can lead to low self-worth, depressive and anxiety disorders, high stress in the face of failure, and even suicidality." It seems that perfectionism is not the asset we might believe it to be; on the contrary, it may be the thing that keeps us from living our best lives. Dr. Brown puts it simply: "Perfection is a twenty-ton shield that we lug around thinking it will protect us when, in fact, it's the thing that's really preventing us from taking flight."

Amen, sister. And if we're constantly worried about how others might perceive us or our interests, then how can we possibly live with our whole selves?

I was quickly discovering that all signs seem to point to a simple truth: Being an amateur might just be good for our brains. As proof, consider a study, published in 2023, in which researchers found that people who pursued hobbies reported better health, more happiness, fewer symptoms of depression, and higher life satisfaction than those who didn't. It appears that by rejecting perfectionism and hustle culture, and instead embracing a practice purely for enjoyment's sake, it's possible to live happier and healthier lives. *Intentional* amateurism, in other words, could just be the secret sauce to a merry soul.

Consider also the words of art historian Dr. Sarah Lewis, whose book *The Rise* explores how our most creative endeavors evolve from failed attempts. She distinguishes the "apprentice" from what she calls a "deliberate amateur," writing, "Deliberate amateurs are not trying to follow an apprentice's schedule—learn the trade, climb the guild's rungs, train another." For this reason, Dr. Lewis explains, the amateur stays in the place of the "constant now," with the benefit of "seeing possibilities to which the expert is blind and which the apprentice may not yet discern." She continues: "An amateur's adventure is an embodied feeling of being rapt, utterly absorbed."

My friend Jenn Romolini is a testament to this: An award-winning author, editor, and media consultant, she's also the cohost of the popular podcast, *Everything Is Fine*. I met Jenn while promoting my book *Radiant Rebellion: Reclaim Aging, Practice Joy, and Raise a Little Hell* and was lucky enough to be interviewed by her. After recording stopped, she and I kept chatting, and our conversation turned to amateurism. She mentioned that she had taken up weaving wall hangings. And, according to her, she's really bad at it.

"No, seriously, I'm awful," she grinned. "Like, my weavings are *ugly*. My goal is to make them beautiful, but right now they're truly not great. I haven't figured out what colors look good together. There are so many techniques that I don't know how to do. I have furry parts where there shouldn't be furry parts."

"And yet you love doing it," I said.

"I *love* doing it," she agreed, her eyes sparkling. The misplaced furry parts didn't seem to dim her delight one iota.

For the record, I totally related to her joy: In my own amateur photography practice, the fact that my efforts occasionally result in an underexposed or blurry image never discourages me—sometimes it even delights me. When, years ago, I decided to take up knitting, I was surprised at how soothing the process became. I was elated when I finally made a sweater my toddler daughter could actually wear—never mind that one arm was longer than the other. (The sweater had different arm lengths, not my daughter. Her arms are the same length.) Even my Hula-Hoop practice—arguably the most amateur of my pursuits—can result in total rapture, especially if it's beautiful outside, and even more especially if I'm hooping to a new Beyoncé album. And all this joy arises by mere happenstance. Imagine what could happen if I put a bit of deliberation behind my amateurism!

Frankly, being a total amateur—and an *intentional* one—was beginning to sound like a magical way to live.

While I've clearly spent a lifetime being less-than-perfect (with a trail of ephemera that includes warped Hula-Hoops, dark or blurry photos, and ill-fitting sweaters as evidence), all joyful and healthful benefits of my amateurism had come about mostly from dumb luck. I was beginning to realize that I hadn't practiced amateurism with any intentionality—and that perhaps it was time to do so. Dabbling—defined as trying an activity for a short period—might be the perfect way to help me discover what new potential avocations I might love. What if I dabbled in a few new activities (or returned to a few old ones) as a way of dipping my toes in the water, a first step to resisting the relentless messages of productivity? What if I tinkered with a few new side interests with the intent of exploring what I love to do, not for the sake of making money or even becoming proficient at them, but simply for the joy of doing them? What if I deliberately suppressed the urge to become an expert or a master? What if I actually *tried* to become . . . well, a total amateur?

Deep down, I knew that intentional amateurism wasn't going to be easy. My daily schedule often feels too full to contemplate the idea of enjoying anything simply for the sake of enjoying it. Besides, I also tend to throw myself into a project and go great guns to the point of burnout (hello, every single New Year's resolution I've ever attempted). If I was going to do this, I didn't want to repeat that disillusioning pattern. But with the research suggesting that making the time for intentional amateurism would be beneficial for my well-being, I figured it was worth the try.

Because the pursuit of amateurism is such unexplored terrain, I decided I would identify what I considered the attributes of intentional amateurism and use them as guidelines for making the practice sustainable. After a lifetime of believing in the conventional wisdom to excel—whether at school or at work or at parenting or, let's face it, at *living*—I hoped that using these attributes as a protocol would help me embark on this experiment in a healthy way. Besides, having this scaffolding would also ensure that I didn't get too timid about pushing myself, for fear of failing or looking like a fool. There was no reason to be concerned about "failing" at any of this—because, honestly, failure is part of the point. My aim wasn't to practice intentional amateurism *perfectly*; it was just to *practice* it. If, through trial and error or sheer stubborn persistence, I actually did get better at a task, that would simply be a by-product—never the goal.

And so, these Seven Attributes of Intentional Amateurism served as my North Star while I explored the activities that I would purposely *not* excel at. We'll look at these in more detail in subsequent chapters.

1. *Curiosity.* When I was writing my book *Radiant Rebellion*, I interviewed dozens of folks who embrace getting older. To a person, they cited curiosity as the secret to joy-filled living. Curiosity opens portals to understanding our gifts and skills, and it even illuminates the values core to who we are. I know this to be true in my own life: Some of the most fulfilling and fun things I've ever done, from law school to Hula-Hooping, happened because I was curious. Fashion designer Norma Kamali says it best: "This is what happens when you make room in your life for curiosity and adventure: Doors open to worlds you never imagined."

Curiosity had to be key to intentional amateurism, as well. I wasn't going to embark on any activities that didn't sound interesting or fun to me, or ones that I wasn't curious about. This was not the time for "should-do" tasks like "lose twenty pounds" or "eat better." This experiment would be all about the purely fun things that pique my interest now, or those that have piqued it in the past.

2. *Mindfulness.* My life is an exercise in freneticism: I'm often on a plane, traveling to do a keynote or lead a workshop, which allows precious little time to rest. My calendar is scheduled to the hilt. If I'm not working to a deadline, I'm catching up on what was ignored while I was working to that deadline. I'm also an incredibly impatient person: Driving behind someone going slowly makes my eye twitch. If the person ahead of me in security doesn't realize that they're supposed to remove their laptop from their carry-on, I have to take deep breaths to maintain my cool. To say that I could do with learning a bit about patience is an understatement.

So as I considered activities to practice amateurism, it seemed like a chance to also practice patience in the form of mindfulness: to seek activities requiring methodical and deliberate actions, and to find opportunities to make intentional, unemotional responses. Patience and mindfulness require slowing down, focusing on each moment as it's happening. And the best part is that even outside of acknowledged mindfulness-cultivating activities like yoga and meditation, so many avocations require slow concentration: spending time tending a garden, for example. Or making complicated pastry. Or even painting. So for the purposes of this experiment, I wanted to look for opportunities to cultivate a practice of enjoying more of the "during-experience," and focusing less on the end product.

3. *Self-Compassion.* I assumed "detachment of ego" would be chief among the attributes of intentional amateurism. After all, amateurism, at its heart, should be an exercise in keeping our egos in check. I knew detaching myself from my ego wasn't going to be easy: When we're conditioned to excel at what we do, any time we fall short, it's discouraging. And what, we're just supposed to . . . stop being discouraged? That's just not how feelings work. Instead, I realized I needed to learn how to deal with discouragement so that I felt safe, calm, and focused enough to keep going after any setbacks.

Happily, I came across Dr. Kristin Neff, a professor whose work is focused on the concept of self-compassion. Her groundbreaking work argues that self-compassion can be far more powerful than continuously striving to maintain high self-esteem. She writes: "When we're mainly filtering our experience through the ego, constantly trying to improve or maintain our high self-esteem, we're denying ourselves the thing we actually want most. To be accepted as we are, an integral part of something much greater than our small selves. Unbounded. Immeasurable. Free." In practicing self-compassion, it's possible to make the experience of our avocations transcendent. While amateurism is never about mastery, there's no reason why its self-compassionate practice can't lift the soul.

4. *Play*. Amateurism is best when it allows for experimentation and play: Once you've learned the basics, you follow your curiosity and see where it leads. For example, decades ago when I first began to practice photography, I had no intention of being any good. In fact, I assumed that I would *never* be good at it. I'd grown up believing that I was more analytical than artistic, but I figured I'd give photography a whirl. After all, since a camera is a machine and I had an engineering degree, surely I could figure it out, right? I purchased a new-to-me-second-hand camera, and my photographer friend, Josef, offered to show me how to use it. After a few hours of teaching me about ISOs and depth of field, he left me to my own devices: I was now free to experiment to my heart's content. Eventually, I learned how to use the camera settings to bend the light to my will. I discovered how to tell a story through imagery. I was free to *play*.

And that freedom is why, decades later, I still love photography. So for this amateurism project, I wanted to recapture that sense of freedom and play. I suspected this would be the key to longevity in its practice.

5. *Stretch Zone*. I am a deeply risk-averse person. You will never see me diving off a cliff, or jumping out of a perfectly good airplane, or test-driving a race car on a closed circuit. It's just not going to happen.

But there's no denying the research indicating that stretching our comfort zones can be good for us, for reasons including potentially lowering our risk of depression, supporting personal growth, and increasing our adaptability. This certainly was the case for me when I learned how to scuba dive, or when I first danced at Carnival in the streets of Trinidad wearing nothing more than a bikini, or even when I decided to become a parent. In all those circumstances, I was terrified to try, but thrilled once I did. Finding opportunities to expand my comfort zone seemed like an obvious move toward intentional amateurship. The saying goes that life begins at the end of our comfort zone. The way I figured it, as I embarked on this exploration into amateurism, I might as well find out where the edge of my comfort zone actually was.

6. *Connection.* I'm starting to think that doing things purely for the purpose of sharing them on the internet might not be good for us. (I realize that this is rich coming from someone who has maintained an online presence for over twenty years.) I say this not just because it's exhausting to continuously create content to feed social media algorithms, but also because I can't help but feel worse for the wear when I'm caught in an endless loop of scrolling. There's research that indicates why this is: In his book *The Perfection Trap*, psychologist and behavioral scientist Dr. Thomas Curran maintains that the "epidemic" of our global grappling with perfectionism is spurred on by "widescreen televisions, tablets and smartphones projecting unrealistic ideals at us 24/7, and social media platforms, with their Photoshopped images of perfection ubiquitous, occupying almost a quarter of our waking

existence." *Yeesh.* And columnist Arthur Brooks describes the inevitable result on our collective psyche bluntly: "Social media threatens to make every slip-up an extinction-level event, socially and professionally." Every time we share online, it adds to the cacophony of perfectionism . . . is this *really* how we want to live our lives?

Here's a different approach: Rather than considering how what we're doing could make good content for the 'gram, what if, instead, we tried new things and shared them solely for the purpose of connection? We could join *offline* communities, or share our avocations solely with loved ones, or photograph our pursuits purely for our own future private enjoyment and reflection. Or—stay with me now—*not photograph them at all.* For this exercise in intentional amateurism, I decided to focus on a few activities whose primary purpose would be connection and collaboration, not publicity and amplification. These would be experiments in focusing on relationships *off*line, rather than trying to present an image of perfection *on*line.

7. *Wonder and Awe.* I was curious: In a time that seems more disconnected and cynical than ever, would it be possible to use intentional amateurism as a tool to become reenchanted with the world—and in so doing, tap into feelings of wonder and awe? Like the other attributes, awe is good for our well-being—and potentially the well-being of the planet, too. Psychology professor Dacher Keltner's research certainly seems to indicate as much. "While experiencing awe," he explains,

"the parts of our brains that are associated with our ego, such as self-criticism, anxiety and depression, 'quiet down,' we shift from a competitive dog-eat-dog mindset to perceive that we are part of networks of more interdependent, collaborating individuals."

Imagine if our practice of amateurism could make us kinder, more interconnected, and more considerate! So for this final attribute, I intended to find something I could do to both inspire joy and also wonder, moving me to explore my own place in the universe.

The time had come to pay attention to myself, to learn not what I could master but instead to enjoy what I enjoy. To learn what I love, and to love it well. Pure intent, open mind, passionate interest: This book chronicles what happened when I became recommitted to the art of amateurship. I used the Seven Attributes of Intentional Amateurism to help me to stay in the "constant now," reducing the chance that I'd succumb to stressors and societal expectations of excellence. It is a sometimes real-time journal of rediscovering what I love. I include interviews with folks who never forgot how to be interesting; they share stories about how they experiment and explore their own comfort zone's edge. These are folks who return to childhood passions and go on brave adventures. And of course, I reveal which of my own experiments have resulted in new avocations: activities outside of work I'll likely do for many years to come, whether I eventually achieve mastery in them or not.

Austin Kleon, an expert on creativity in the modern world, writes, "If you want to change your life, change what you pay attention to." I hope, as you read these pages, you come along with me in the journey to shift our focus away from expertise and perfection, and instead concentrate on the embodied enjoyment of doing what we love. Practicing each of the attributes along the way, let's remind ourselves how to be interesting again, if only for our own personal fulfillment and growth. Consider the ways that you can try activities that allow you to practice mindfulness. Dabble in new hobbies to determine which ones activate your curiosity. Stretch your comfort zone. Maybe even cultivate everyday awe.

In other words, make time to delight yourself.

It's time to embrace the brilliance of being a total amateur.

2

The Spirituality of Intentional Amateurism and the Making of an Amateur's Menu

WHEN I DECIDED to embark on this adventure of intentional amateurism, I did what most people would do in this age of digital connectivity. Without a second thought (and in full violation of Attribute #6), I announced my intentions publicly. I told anyone who would listen—family, friends, even online strangers—what I was about to do. "I'm going to become a total amateur, *on purpose*," I would say. "I have no idea whether the dabbling I'm about to do will lead to a discovery of my next avocational passion or will result in my falling flat on my face. But *here I go*."

Everyone was very supportive. "How fun!" they'd respond. "I can't wait to hear how it turns out." But inevitably, I also heard many stories explaining why it was impossible for them to do anything similar: The idea of cultivating hobbies or even dabbling in new adventures seemed akin to planning a trip to Venus. More than one person wrote to me privately: "I *used* to have hobbies," they'd say, "but I don't anymore.

Parenting and work *drain* me. Any spare time I have I really just want to spend *sleeping*."

Boy, do I get this. It was all very well and good to proclaim that I was going to embark on a search for an avocation to do in my downtime; it was entirely another thing to *find* the downtime required to do it. How, exactly, are we supposed to pack more things to do into our already busy lives?

The short answer? Intentional amateurism should *never* feel like a chore; it should feel like self-care. It isn't supposed to feel like a *have*-to-do, but rather, a *get*-to-do. Ideally, it shouldn't feel like work. It should feel like rest. And I've come to believe that rest and leisure are paramount to thriving.

When I wrote my book *The Lightmaker's Manifesto: How to Work for Change Without Losing Your Joy*, I interviewed about a dozen activists who dedicate their time to making the world better and who manage to do so without losing heart. They all agree: The only way—and I mean, the *only* way—to cultivate longevity in activism is to have a cadence of self-care. As I internalized their collective wisdom, I realized that what's true for activism is also true for life: The only way to thrive in a world that is full of challenges and responsibilities is to build rest and leisure into our lives. And just as the seasons turn, the moon waxes and wanes, and the tides rise and fall, rest and leisure should be a rhythmic part of every day.

This concept is echoed by Tricia Hersey, a poet, performance artist, activist, and author. Her best-selling book, *Rest is Resistance: A Manifesto*, makes a compelling case for the rejection of hustle culture, or what she calls, "grind culture." She argues that we've all been brainwashed by capitalism and that we believe our worthiness resides in how much we produce. Instead, she argues, we should center rest and leisure in our lives. "You don't have to always be creating, doing and contributing to the world," she writes. "Your birth grants you rest and leisure, as well." Hersey's manifesto asserts that with the ever-present pressure to produce, making a conscious effort to unplug from hustle culture is, in itself, a radical act of self-compassion. "Rest is radical because it disrupts the lie that we are not doing enough," she explains. "It shouts, 'No, that is a lie! I am enough. I am worthy now and always because I am here.'"

Hersey's words are also an exhortation to remember that ultimately, we are not meant to live as cogs in a capitalistic machine, but rather, we are spiritual beings navigating a material world. Remembering this opens us to the limitless possibilities of rest and leisure being *spiritual* practices, ones that can be woven into the fabric of our lives, in a rhythmic form of self-care. Is it possible that viewing our leisurely pursuits and avocations through this lens could transform them from being responsibilities that require our attention, to activities that energize us, bringing us peace and calm, or even exhilaration and joy? Could doing these activities—these practices of intentional amateurism—help us build our reserves for handling the responsibilities of our lives, especially if we did so in a rhythmic, even ritualistic manner?

I'd argue this is exactly the purpose of our intentional amateurism.

Casper ter Kuile is a writer and podcaster who holds master's degrees in both divinity and public policy from Harvard University. His book, *The Power of Ritual*, explores how we can nourish our souls by transforming everyday practices into sacred rituals, in some ways creating a foundation for our spiritual lives. In his book, he tells the story of a serious accident in which he fell from a pier and broke both his legs and his wrist and double-fractured his spine. His recovery required weeks in the hospital and months in a wheelchair. At the time of his accident, he was a young man just out of university, and this new life was a shock: "Instead of juggling meetings, calls and emails," he writes, "the major event of my day became a trip to the shower, carried up the stairs by my father and sister." Needless to say, the experience left him demoralized.

In the months of recovery after his fall, however, ter Kuile's mother invited an artist friend of hers to stop by his home every week to paint with him. Ter Kuile had no artistic experience, and he describes how hesitant he was to paint with his mother's friend. "Nothing frustrates me more than failing in public," he writes. But he agreed, and discovered that this new pastime provided more than just the opportunity to improve his art skills. It also provided him a way to process his accident and integrate the experience into the person he had become as a result. He writes: "This experience of seeing how a supposedly secular practice like painting could become a powerful, perhaps even spiritual way of connecting to myself made me realize that there were other small, seemingly insignificant habits that did the same thing."

According to ter Kuile, anything can become a spiritual practice, as long as we're clear about our intention in doing the activity. By asking ourselves "What am I inviting to this moment?" we bring our attention and presence to the activity and commit to returning to the practice of the activity time and time again. "In this way," he asserts, "rituals make the invisible connections that make life meaningful, visible."

Given that leisure is our birthright and that the practice of leisure activities in a ritualistic way can be a spiritual practice, intentional amateurism has the potential to be a powerful form of self-care. And the beauty of this is that any activity we choose as a potential avocation—whether it involves returning to a past passion or dabbling in something new—could be a perfect candidate for this restful, restorative practice.

Now, confident that this pursuit of intentional amateurism could only help enhance my life and energize me for my day-to-day responsibilities, I found that only one question remained: What activities should I try?

The secret to becoming a committed amateur is cultivating a mindset that leaves you open to possibilities, encourages self-compassion, and releases you from the drive to succeed. Intentional amateurship also calls for the ability to discern the difference between what society tells you is supposed to feel fun and what *actually* feels fun—a skill that requires curiosity and considerable self-knowledge. So even though I had established the Seven Attributes of Intentional Amateurism, the time had come to determine what activities I could experiment with. Obviously, photography was something that I already enjoyed and that I could revive in a new way; but beyond that, I didn't really have many other hobbies or interests. I needed to figure out what else I could try: things that I love and comfortably pursue without intending mastery.

As I mulled this question, I remembered a friend of mine with whom I'd lost touch: Maggie Mason, a writer and early blogging pioneer I'd met almost two decades earlier when I'd first started writing. Back then, Maggie had extolled the virtues of what she called a "Life List," which she said is "a less-morbid version of a bucket list." While a bucket list is about checking off activities before your inevitable demise, the idea behind the Life List was to create a list of activities that would add *more* life to your life—activities that, every December 31st, would remind you to marvel at how much you'd simply enjoyed living the previous year.

Maggie's Life List became a viral internet sensation, and hundreds of people around the world (myself included) began sharing our own life lists online. The activities that folks were attempting varied wildly and included learning how to hula dance, trying a new recipe every week, and the fairly creepy one of finding a celebrity to kiss.

It struck me now that Maggie's Life List exercise overlapped with what I wanted to do with my own in intentional amateurism, although her list (and those of others who emulated her) mostly included once-and-done types of activities. But perhaps I could develop a similar list, just one that focused on *practices*. Such a list—a menu of options, so to speak—could help to steer me toward a life of intentional amateurism.

I reached out to Maggie, to ask her how she came up with her Life List idea in the first place, and what, in retrospect, she felt like the list had added to her life. Happily, she agreed. So one hot summer day, we connected over Zoom and I asked her to help me understand how she went about creating hers.

She laughed. "It's not a super-complex concept."

I smiled. "It's not, but I know when I was creating mine, I needed to come up with a few rules to make it happen in a way that worked for me. And I'm sure it was the same for you, yes?"

"Yes. And there was definitely a lot of trial and error to come up with them."

"Exactly. So first things first: When did you come up with the idea of making this list for yourself?"

"Well, I've kept journals all my life," she began, "and I've always been a list person. In fact, in college I wrote a humor column called The List, which was just a series of lists of jokes with one unifying idea, like about being drunk, or spring break, or whatever college-related thing I could think of. After college, I kept writing lists in my journal: I'd be sitting in front of the television and write things down that I wanted to do with my life. These lists would inspire subsets. So I'd write down things like 'I want to see one hundred countries,' or 'when I'm old, I want to go to the moon.' Then I'd make a subset: 'things I'd need to do to go to the moon.' And so on. As an editor and a writer, I'd think of these lists as sort of a narrative exercise.

"Eventually, after I'd been blogging for several years, I pulled out all the lists and little notes I'd kept over my life. Using them, I created the first true iteration of the Life List and started blogging about it. As it happened, at the time I was with an agency who helped me find sponsors to make items on the list happen."

"I remember that," I said. "Some of those activities were incredible. There was some international travel involved, dare-devil activities—crazy experiences!"

"They were." She grinned. "It was an intense time that taught me a lot."

I asked her for an example. "Well, for one thing, one of my goals in doing my Life List was to expand my fear horizon. And one of the tech sponsors required that I do a lot of what I call 'adventure-helmet' activities, because those make for the most exciting photos. So here I was, signed up to do adventure-helmet things, when I'm a person who wants to read a book in the bathtub with a cup of tea. But I'm being paid, right? So I had no choice."

"At the time, one of the things on my Life List was parasailing, but we couldn't find anywhere to do it. So as an alternative, my husband booked someone who could take me para*gliding*. I had no idea what paragliding was."

"Uh oh."

"But I'm committed to doing it, so off I go. On the way, I'm researching what I'm getting into, and I read on my phone, 'parasailing and paragliding are often confused.' Turns out that one of them is a carnival ride and suitable for children. The other is an adventure sport that prevents you from getting life insurance."

"Let me guess," I grinned. "You weren't signed up for the carnival ride."

"*Exactly*. So we get there, and the weather's not cooperating. And while we're waiting for the weather to abate, everything in my body is telling me I shouldn't do this. But all these social pressures are coming in on me: *This guy doesn't get paid if I don't do this. I need the content for my blog. I have to do this.*

"Eventually the guy suggests that we go higher to try to avoid the weather. We keep going higher and higher, and I'm noticing how much higher the cliff is that I'm eventually going to have to jump off. Finally, I can't take it anymore. I declare out loud, 'I'm not doing this.'"

"You called it!"

"Yeah, I called it. I totally backed out. But for months after, the fear stayed with me—it made me more scared to try *anything*. Finally, one day, a friend insisted I go para*sailing* with her. We were in Austin for a conference, and I took some convincing, but eventually, I relented. During some off time, we went parasailing over a lake. It was *beautiful*. It felt like how everything feels when it's in flow."

Maggie leaned in to make sure I understood. "So it turns out that I'm a para*sailing* girl, but I'm *not* a para*gliding* girl. And the whole experience taught me that I didn't have to just check things off my list to be the kind of person I perceived the world wants me to be—not if I don't want to be that person. It's totally fine to be the kind of person who reads books in the bathtub with a cup of tea. I can stretch myself, but only to my *own* definition of what's brave."

This seemed like an incredibly important lesson: Because of our societal conditioning to constantly achieve, when we decide to pursue something as an amateur, it can feel defeatist to choose activities we believe aren't daring or cool. Granted, Maggie's situation was different—as an influencer, she was being paid to do her activities—but this doesn't negate the fact that we all internalize pressures to achieve to the standards we believe society sets for us.

I made a note to remember this as I came up with amateurism activities. Whether they inspired calm or courage, I needed to ask myself: *Is this really something I want to do? Does doing this sound fun? Is there a likelihood it will bring me joy?*

"Were there any activities that you were happy to try, even though they felt scary?" I asked Maggie.

"Well, one thing on my list was to learn how to roll a kayak."

"Okay, see, this sounds terrifying," I said. "But I totally remember you doing this and asking you why you would even consider doing such a thing."

She grinned. "Oh, I was nervous about rolling the kayak," she said. "But at the time, I remember thinking that I was afraid of a lot of things that I didn't need to be afraid of. Even though I was anxious about rolling the kayak, unlike paragliding, I wasn't afraid for my *life*. Like, I *like* kayaking. I go kayaking a lot. If the kayak flipped, I knew I could get out of it one way or another. It wouldn't be the end of the world. But with paragliding, in my mind the worst thing that could happen would be *actual death*. Why would I do that? I realized that I didn't need to put that on my list just because I wanted to be the badass who jumped off a cliff."

Maggie's decision to learn how to a roll a kayak is an excellent lesson in discernment. In this case, she flirted with the edge of her comfort zone: She was nervous, she said, but also already had experience in maneuvering a kayak. She was determined to stretch herself, knowing she had a tendency to fear things she needn't fear. This is the kind of mindful self-inquiry we would all benefit from before beginning our own intentional amateurism experiments.

We talked for a bit longer, and she shared a few of her philosophies about how to make a list. She mentioned her belief that it should always be written down, not just a list in your head ("because you have all these things at the back of your mind that you've always wanted to do, but you can never remember them in the moment"). She also discussed the importance of focusing on yourself ("your list items should be about what *you* want, not what you want for other people—they can make their own lists"). These all made total sense to me, and I began to get excited about what I could do to adapt my own list to pursue my exploration into amateurism.

"What's the biggest piece of advice you would give someone who is developing a list of things they might want to dabble in?"

"Well," she began, "I think the biggest mistake folks make is believing that because they've made a list, they must do *everything on the list.* There's absolutely no compromise, and if they don't do a certain number within a certain amount of time, they give up."

"I could see that," I said, nodding grimly. "Perfectionism is a hell of a drug."

"Exactly. So my advice would be to remember your list is a living document. You don't write your list in blood. You can add things whenever you want, but also, they don't have to remain on your list forever. You make the rules. Cut yourself a break."

After our conversation, I pulled out my journal to think about my own list. What could I do to ensure that it both adds life to my life, but also keeps me from crossing over into burnout or perfectionism? I resisted putting "be sure you know the difference between carnival rides and adventure sports" at the very top of the page. And then I began writing.

I knew that creating a list that speaks to my intentional amateur's heart needed to be diverse enough to spark imagination, but realistic enough for me to put into some sort of practice. My list would be different from Maggie's. Unlike hers, I didn't want my list to be an inventory of singular events or include opportunities that are only of the mondo-beyondo-once-in-a-lifetime ilk. That's not to say that I didn't want to dabble in practices that nudge me out of my comfort zone. But in all cases, I wanted them to be activities I was hoping to put some practice into, ones that would inspire my own self-care and self-compassion in the process. Accessible activities that would add moments of joy to my life. Moments of *light*. And I wanted this to be more of a *menu*: a list of items from which I could simply pick and choose what sounded interesting, rather than feeling compelled to try them all.

And so, with this in mind, I set out to create my Amateur's Menu. As I began, I found that a few questions were helpful to kick-start my brainstorming. I share them here, in the hopes that perhaps you will too, as you embark on your own Intentional Amateurism project.

First, *what did you love to do as a kid?* Think about any hobbies that you used to have: sports you played, crafts you made. Was there something that your mom had to beg you to stop doing so you could come to the kitchen to join your family for dinner? That's a clue that this activity might belong on your menu.

Also: Consider those activities that you did in your childhood that might have been thought of as quirks, but that, on deeper evaluation, indicate an underlying passion. For example, ever since I was a kid, I've had a thing for handwriting. I used to change my handwriting constantly. I'd pore through books and old writing practice texts, looking for all the different ways I could print an *a* or a *g* or a cursive *r*. I redesigned the way I signed notes so often that you can tell how old I was when I wrote any given letter by my signature alone.

Now, most would assume that this was the obsession of a young girl, and I'd outgrown it years ago. But the truth is that I still play with letters, all the time. I have a Pinterest board full of hand-lettering inspiration. Most nights I practice in a journal, as a way to wind down my day and bring a bit of calm to my evenings. I even played with lettering while writing this book: You can see my amateurish experiments on the introduction pages of each chapter. I've no desire to be a professional calligrapher, nor can I fully explain why making letters makes me so happy, but it does.

So think about those things that you loved to do that may not quite have risen to the level of "hobby" in your mind, and see if there's something more to them. Did you constantly rearrange your bedroom when you were a kid? Perhaps an avocation in interior design awaits. Loved to line up dominoes just to watch them tumble? Maybe you have a Rube Goldberg–machine designer inside of you, crying to get out. Follow your curiosity, and delight in where it leads you.

Second, ask yourself *what would you do if you were ten years younger*? Or, *what would you do if you were ten years older*? This might seem like a strange question, but in his book, *The Power of Regret: How Looking Backward Moves Us Forward*, author Daniel Pink shares one of his most robust findings: Over time, we are much more likely to have *boldness regret*—regret over the chances we *didn't* take—than regret about the chances we did. "With boldness regrets," he writes, "we choose to play it safe. That may relieve us, at first. The chance we're contemplating may sound too big, too disruptive, too challenging, too hard. But eventually the choice distresses us with a counterfactual in which we were more daring, and consequently, more fulfilled. Boldness regrets sound like this: *if only I'd taken that risk*."

Intentional amateurism encourages us to take that risk, but with a crucial safety net: *You don't have to be good at it*. In fact, no one needs to know that you're trying it, if you don't want them to. So consider the things you always wished you'd tried, but didn't, or the activities that you wonder if you're "too old" (whatever that means) to try now. Or, in the alternative:

Think about the things you think would make Future You one of the most interesting older people on the block. And then, *go do them.* You just might fall deeper in love with your life because you did.

Third, consider *what talent you wish you had.* My brother-in-law, John, is a skilled blues guitarist, but he's never played a single concert. An attorney by trade, he had always been interested in learning how to play. One year he received guitar lessons as a Father's Day gift. It's been over twenty years, and he's still taking weekly lessons. "I like having regular lessons for a number of reasons," he told me. "First, in order to improve and make time to play and practice, it helps me to have an appointment and a commitment to my teacher to do it. Even if I haven't had time to practice much during the week, forty minutes or so before my lesson keeps me on the right track."

"But also," he continued, "I like that there are no real demands or deadlines for learning the guitar—unlike in the rest of my life. My teacher and I just keep working on a piece until we're both pretty satisfied with it, or we find something we're more interested in attempting. And after twenty years, my teacher has become my friend. We really enjoy each other's company, and it's fun to hang out once a week and talk about both guitar and non-guitar things."

John's intentional amateurism practice hasn't just made him a wonderful guitarist (which, by the way, benefits the rest of our family immensely, in the form of the impromptu jam sessions that occur when we get together). It's also brought self-compassion, mindfulness, and even connection into his life. So, wish you could sing like Maria Callas? Consider taking voice lessons, even if you've never sung before, even if you can't carry a tune in a basket. Dream of being a master of martial arts? Look up that capoeira studio in your neighborhood. Remember, this is just for you and your own enjoyment. There's no reason for anyone to know about the secret superpower you're cultivating.

Fourthly, ask yourself: *What did you do on your most playful vacation?* Often, the things we do during our time off that we enjoy the most are clues to the kinds of hobbies that would make for a good amateurism practice. For example, did you go camping for the first time and love it? Perhaps it's time to tap into your inner outdoorsman and begin a monthly practice of camping. Did you learn to make pasta on your trip to Rome and surprise yourself at how much you enjoyed it? Maybe there's a future in cooking your family authentic Italian meals. Chances are that what you did during your times off provided a glimpse into the joy that you could begin folding into your daily life. So pull out those photos you took on those vacations and see what nuggets of bliss you find.

Finally, *what types of social media content do you follow?* If you're like me, you follow folks who create content by doing things you only fantasize about. (In my case, I follow people who enhance their homes with DIY construction, chefs, globe makers, shoemakers, gardeners, bartenders—all who engage in activities I have not done . . . yet.) The people who intrigue you online can inspire you into a new hobby you just might fall in love with.

Answer these five questions, and you'll have a good start on creating your own intentional amateurism menu. And for more inspiration, check out the Abridged List of Things I Tried and Didn't Try (but Still Might) at the end of this book. Read each item out loud, and if you find that your heart jumps at any one of them, add it to your menu.

Here's my point: One of my favorite movies our family used to watch when our daughter was little is *Mr. Magorium's Wonder Emporium*. It's the tale of a young woman named Molly Mahoney (played by the utterly charming Natalie Portman). Mahoney (as she's called in the movie) is a former musical child prodigy and an amateur pianist who is suffering from artist's block. By day, she works as the manager of Mr. Magorium's Wonder Emporium, a magical toy store owned by 243-year-old Mr. Magorium (played by the enchanting Dustin Hoffman). The story is about how Mahoney finds her "sparkle." But my favorite scene—perhaps my favorite movie scene of all time—is near the end of movie, when Mr. Magorium is saying goodbye to Mahoney before he departs (transcends?). He grabs her by both hands, looks deep into her eyes, and says:

> *"Your life is an occasion. Rise to it."*

This is ultimately the purpose of intentional amateurism and the true utility of the Amateur's Menu: to provide the inspiration to rise to your life's occasion. The reason for making this list, and for carving out the time to do activities that refill your spirit in a predictable cadence, is to ensure you're living your life, with all its challenges and responsibilities, as joyfully as possible. Because we can never infuse our lives with too much joy and light, and as a dear friend of mine once told me: "It's in the living that we create a life."

As for me, more than fifty activities eventually comprised my Amateur's Menu, and I certainly could have kept going. (Again, you can find many of the ones that made my list, as well as a few others that would never be on my list, but might make yours, at the back of this book.) So for the remainder of this book, I share with you what happened as I dabbled in a few of them: where I succeeded, where I failed, but mostly, what I learned about myself in the process. I also share which ones are likely to become a part of my amateur practice going forward.

But the truth is that whether they become a part of the fabric of my life story, or they're simply discarded threads along the way, just having spent the effort to explore what I love, care for myself, and maybe even stretch a little is all the reward that counts.

curiosity

Curiosity

Failure Is Fascinating

WHEN I WAS five years old, my family and I lived in Guayaguayare, a small fishing village in my homeland, the Caribbean island of Trinidad. Dad worked as a production engineer at the Amoco Oil facility at Galeota Point, the southeasternmost corner of the country. I attended Amoco Galeota School, the tiny private school that Amoco Oil had established for the children of American expatriates, as well as the kids of local Trinidadian employees who worked at "Point." The school was relatively new, and there were only a handful of students. Ms. Saunders, the kindergarten teacher, was a local Trinidadian with a smile like sunshine, belying a true no-nonsense attitude. I adored her.

The school had limited resources, but made magic with what it had. Its biggest asset was its engaged parent community, so when Ms. Saunders suggested that the entire school have a cultural visit to a local potter in the nearby town of Rio Claro, everyone's mom eagerly offered to carpool all of us there.

The history of pottery in Trinidad is quite rich. After slavery was abolished, indentured servants from India were brought in by the plantation owners to work the sugar cane fields in the central region of the country. Naturally, these newcomers to the island brought their customs and art forms with them. India has a long tradition of clay pottery, especially wares traditionally used for both household and religious purposes. I grew up with pottery used as home decor, and these days, you can find a lot of Trinidadian pottery in souvenir and gift shops.

But the pottery is most visible during the Hindu festival of Diwali. Then, the faithful decorate their balconies and the eaves of their homes with diyas, candles made with a wick and wax poured into small ceramic, bowl-shaped vessels. Diwali was one of my favorite nights of the year because my parents would drive my sister and me around the village to look at the beautiful, illuminated homes.

Ms. Saunders told us that on this trip to Rio Claro, we would learn how the diyas were made. When the day finally came, we piled into the cars of the parents who showed up to drive us to Rio Claro. (My mom wasn't among them—she had my baby sister at home to take care of.) The cars left the parking lot in a single file led by Ms. Saunders, and we made our way through the coconut groves and banana plantations, deeper and deeper inland before finally arriving at a small, brightly colored clapboard house on stilts. Slowly, shyly, we got out of the cars, as Ms. Saunders went to greet a large woman walking toward us, grinning from ear to ear.

"Hello! Hello! Welcome, come back! Come back!" she called out, and we followed her through a verdant garden to the back of her house, where there was a large shed. We all walked in, our eyes wide.

To our left, on one table made of scrap wood, was a huge pile of diyas—hundreds, maybe thousands of them—all waiting to be put into use for Diwali. To our right were makeshift shelves containing red clay decorative lanterns, vases, bowls, platters, pitchers, and even large planters in neat rows. Just outside of the workshop was a giant pile of clay, moist and dark red, waiting to be turned into art. At the back was a large clay oven, flames roaring. A teenage boy was adding more scrap wood to the fire. And in the middle of all of this was a potter's wheel, at which a man was intently working away.

The man was skinny, dressed in old clothes, and covered in red clay. He was barefoot, his right foot on a pedal connected to a pottery wheel. The wheel was propelled by an engine and a belt, similar to what I'd seen when my dad popped the hood of his car and let me look inside. On the wheel was a lump of clay, and the man was manipulating it with both hands in fluid motions. Like magic, the lump of clay would grow tall . . . taller . . . until the man would push down on the top of the clay, bringing it back to a circular lump. Then, tall again . . . finally, he moved his thumbs to the top of the clay and pressed down, making it hollow, until he could fit his entire hand inside. Using both hands to manipulate the wall of clay, what had been a lump suddenly formed into an elegant vase.

The man released his foot off the pedal, and the wheel stopped spinning. He looked up and grinned. Ms. Saunders and the moms clapped. We followed suit.

"You see, children," said Ms. Saunders, "Mr. Budhlall is a talented potter, able to make just about anything with his hands. He's been doing this for years. Mr. Budhlall, can you please tell the children about your work?"

Mr. Budhlall explained how he learned to create the pottery from his father, who had learned the craft from his father before him. He described how the clay would "speak" to him, telling him what it wanted to be, and his hands followed suit. (I listened closely to the clay, but I didn't hear anything.) And then, thrillingly, he asked if we'd each like to take a try at the wheel.

First up was Meredith, the daughter of American expats, who was in my class. Meredith was blonde, blue-eyed, and a bit of a troublemaker, constantly reprimanded for talking and disrupting class. But not today: Meredith was transfixed by Mr. Budhlall. She hopped up on his stool, and as he pressed the pedal to begin turning the wheel, she placed her hands on the small lump of clay he'd arranged for her. She scowled in deep concentration as she tried to copy what she'd seen Mr. Budhlall do. Finally, even though her piece didn't resemble anything Mr. Budhlall had created, she broke into a grin as he announced:

"Man, dat is an *expert* ashtray!"

Soon we were all clamoring for our turn at the wheel. One by one, we created "expert ashtrays," which Mr. Budhlall allowed us to take home with us. In the cars on the way back, we chattered excitedly about our ashtrays, begging Ms. Saunders to schedule a date to take us back for another visit. The experience was electrifying.

Eventually, I moved away from that simple life in Guayaguayare, always to large cities for my education and career. My expert ashtray sat on my bedside table for years, until one day it went missing—a casualty of a house relocation, I suspect. But I'd occasionally remember Mr. Budhlall and his potter's wheel, and I'd wonder if I'd ever have the opportunity to try my hand at pottery again.

In my busy life—as an engineer, a lawyer, a mother, a writer—it was easy to dismiss these fleeting thoughts as silly or impractical. I knew, after all, that I never wanted to make a living as a potter. Surely there were other more important things in life that deserved my attention.

But what might happen if I tried? Would I be awful at it? Would it be stressful? Would I make a fool of myself? Would I be even worse at it as an adult than I was as a five-year-old?

And perhaps most important of all: *Would I regret it if I did?*

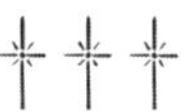

Remember Jenn Romolini, cohost of the *Everything Is Fine* podcast? As I wondered if I could find time to make pottery, I decided to ask her how she gathered up the courage to try her hand at weaving wall hangings. "So what made you begin weaving?" I asked her.

"Well, I've always loved a seventies vibe." She grinned, her eyes crinkling behind decidedly groovy, rose-tinted aviators. "So I enjoy a good woven wall hanging. One day I saw this cool wall hanging that I wanted to buy, but when I looked at the price, it was, like, a thousand dollars. And there was no way I was paying a thousand dollars for *wool knots*. So I had to figure out how to make one myself."

I was skeptical. I mean, while I agree that making a weaving instead of spending a thousand dollars seemed smart, I couldn't help but think it was a pretty bold thing to try. Those wall hangings are *intricate*. "Didn't you have any apprehension about giving it a go?" I asked.

Jenn looked at me like she didn't understand the question. Then she answered: "Well, no. I mean, I think that bravery requires a sense of curiosity about your own mind, you know? Asking yourself, 'What is making me afraid of this? What can't I face? Is it that I would feel too embarrassed and ashamed if I don't know how to do this? What if I can't do it?' and—probably the most important thing to ask yourself—'What's the worst thing that could happen here, and why is this intolerable to me?' Ultimately, I don't like limitations, and I especially don't like *self-imposed* limitations. I feel like the world is going to limit you enough. It seems crazy to limit what you can do in your own mind."

I thought of the apprehension I'd been feeling about looking into pottery. It was suddenly very clear to me that my nervousness was ultimately self-imposed.

"The very first weaving I made took me two months, and it was long, and it was big," Jenn continued. "At the very end, I made a mistake. I loosened all the thread at the top, and it all sort of fell apart and became amorphous. It was so upsetting and disappointing. But it was also *interesting*."

"Interesting? Really?"

"Absolutely." Jenn was emphatic. "It was interesting to see what worked and what didn't. It was interesting to notice my feelings as it fell apart—why were my emotions so strong? It was interesting to experience all these things *when the stakes are nothing*. Failure is *fascinating*."

"Wow," I said. "I never thought of it like that."

"Doing these weavings sparks so much curiosity in me," Jenn continued. "There's something about working through these problems as a creative exercise. They're stimulating in a very visceral, tactile way. Also, when I began weaving, I realized that I enjoyed it more than I'd even imagined. It was something I could do that wasn't commodified; it was pure, and personal. And because I make a living as an artist in other ways, this is a lovely way that I can disentangle money from art."

"I'm so grateful to you for sharing this with me," I said, "because I've been toying with this idea of trying pottery, and I've been a bit stymied about doing it."

"Look, I can only speak for myself," she said. "But I will say that as I look around and I see myself and my peers getting older, we stop wanting to try things. We feel like we know everything, many of us, and we can become more closed as we get older. This is a tragedy. I want to stay open across my whole life. I want to keep experiencing life fully. And when I was younger, one of the ways I did this was seeking out new relationships, trying to find a partner, pushing myself professionally. But then life becomes more settled: I'm with a partner, I have friends, I have a career. So now I look for more opportunities to open my brain, open my heart, *open myself to myself.* The way I figure it, you have to create those opportunities, because they don't come naturally. And creating those opportunities is all about getting curious about my own brain and saying: *What am I interested in? What still scares me? What did I always want to do and thought maybe I couldn't do?* And if you do these things, without a particular goal in mind other than remaining an amateur, it means that it's not scary."

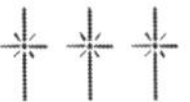

Jenn's encouragement was all I needed to finally take the leap. After some online research, I walked into a ceramics studio for my first lesson.

The facility was pristine—more like a spa than a studio, with immaculate pottery wheels and community tables. A tall, tattooed woman walked over and said, "Can I help you?"

"Um, yes . . ." For some reason, I was speaking in a hushed tone. "I'm here for my appointment. I mean, reservation. I mean . . . class." Why was I so intimidated?

She consulted the iPad on the reservation desk. "Karen?" I nodded. "It looks like you're with Bea today." She pronounced it *BAY-Ah*. "I'll go get her."

As I waited, I wondered what I was getting myself into: I was excited, but also worried that my expectations were outsized. My admiration for Mr. Budhlall remained as strong as ever, but I wondered if my rose-tinted thoughts were those of an adventuresome five-year-old as opposed to an adult who was, let's be honest, somewhat squeamish about getting dirty. Would I be able to let loose and enjoy what would inevitably result in clay under my fingernails?

It was too late to turn around now, as Bea was approaching. "Nice to meet you," she said, extending her hand. "Follow me upstairs."

Bea had a soft accent (I learned she was Argentinean), and although she was smiling, I read her as someone who took her craft very seriously. We arrived on the second floor to find another fleet of tables and wheels. Three other artists were working quietly at their individual stations, each of them in deep concentration.

Bea appraised me with a raised eyebrow.

"You're dressed awfully nicely for this class," she said. Her accent made her seem even more regal to me. "You're going to get dirty."

"Oh, I know," I said, taking off my blazer. "This t-shirt and these jeans are really old. I'm ready."

Satisfied, she nodded. "Okay, put your things here, and follow me."

I did as I was told and joined her at a counter where she was measuring a considerable amount of clay. "First, we have to 'wedge' the clay, to help get rid of any air bubbles and even out its consistency. We begin working the clay like so." She began to knead about a pound of clay. "You see how I'm doing it? You want it to look like this," she paused, "not like this." She paused again, and then returned to kneading. "Like this"—another pause—"See how it looks like a bull's nose? Like that."

I had absolutely no idea what she was talking about. Every time she paused, the clay looked exactly the same, which is to say that at no time did I see a bull's nose. Perhaps I'd never really paid attention to bull noses before. In any event, I didn't want to look dumb. I nodded.

Finally, she took the lump of clay in both hands and said, "It's ready. Let's go to the wheel."

She sat at the wheel, and I sat next to her. "I'm going to show you everything first," she said. "Then you'll try." And with that, she began. She explained what it meant to center the clay, and then used her thumbs to make a hollow in the center. After a moment, she began lifting the walls of the clay, as it magically transformed into a small vessel. As she worked, she spoke.

"Throwing a pot is like life: If you don't make sure that you have the foundation of the piece set, any flaw becomes magnified as you continue to work it," she said. "Just as in life, if you don't have your foundation secure, you're sure to fail going forward. Okay. Now it's your turn."

We traded places, and I looked at the fresh lump of clay that Bea had put on the wheel in front of me. I picked it up and slammed it down on the bat (the small mat on the wheel), as I'd seen her do. She nodded with approval. I pressed the foot pedal, and the wheel began to turn.

"That's a good speed," she said. "Now add a bit of water and try centering the clay."

I began working the clay, surprised at how pleasantly smooth it felt under my hands. I forced the spinning clay into a cone as Bea had illustrated, and then flattened it back down into a cylindrical lump of clay again. I repeated the movement a few more times.

"Okay, good, the clay is now centered," she said. "Now use your thumbs to make the hollow." I did as I was told. "Now, open the hollow." Done. "Great. Now bring up the walls."

I tried to remember how she placed her hands to bring the walls of her bowl up. They started rising, with an almost imperceptible wobble. I prayed she didn't notice.

Bea frowned. "That's . . . so wrong."

Around me there were sudden peals of laughter. I looked up to find the other potters in the room continuing to work on their pieces—while laughing.

"*Damn*," I said, feigning offense. They laughed even harder.

"You know what? You all seem like nice people, but I see now each one of you is cold-blooded."

One of them, a man with a white beard and twinkly eyes, stopped laughing, and looked up from his piece with a grin. "This is the laughter of recognition," he said. "We've all been there."

"Look." Bea reclaimed my attention, holding a wire in her hand. Stunned, I watched as she sliced my piece in half, from top to bottom. Was my work really that bad? "I want to show you something." As she pulled the halves apart, the wobble was obvious: the walls of the pot had an extreme wiggle near their base.

"The clay doesn't lie," Bea said, not without kindness. "See, it tells you exactly where you applied pressure, and where you corrected. It shows you the importance of being constant and steady."

I nodded again. I hadn't even noticed that the pressure I'd been exerting had varied in the least, and I was beginning to understand the true artistry needed to make pottery seem so effortless. Also, I couldn't help but note that the intense dismay I felt when Bea sliced my pot was now replaced by eagerness to give it another go. My emotions had swung from disheartened to determined in *seconds*.

Jenn was right: failure *is* fascinating.

"Let's try again."

For the rest of my lesson, Bea patiently pointed out how to hold my fingers and encouraged me to pay attention to the feel of the clay. "Close your eyes," she said, more than once. "The clay speaks. Use your hands to listen." I remembered how Mr. Budhlall had said the same thing. "You'll know when it's working. It's like when you ride your bike, and you're straining so you change the gear, and suddenly you feel ease," Bea explained. "It's the same with the clay: You'll feel resistance, so you change the pressure. Just wait for the sudden ease."

By the end of our session, I had created two small bowls. "We'll glaze them for you," said Bea. "These are good. And you had an open attitude—that is the most important part of wheel-throwing. Remember, the clay reads your attitude."

A few weeks later, I returned to the studio to pick up my finished pieces. Now glazed, their flaws seemed magnified: My green pot had a bulge around its middle, and my blue pot leaned a little bit. I showed them to a friend of mine. "Have you *ever* seen more wonky pots?"

"They're great," he said. My friend is a very kind man.

"I mean, 'great' is strong," I laughed.

"No, I mean it," he said. "I used to work at a community college as a ceramics lab tech for two years. Trust me when I say I saw a lot of first pieces, and these are great.

"By the way," he continued, "in the ceramics world, the word we use instead of 'wonky' is 'charm.' And it's never a 'flaw'; it's always 'character.' As in, 'I made a lot of charming pieces with character when I was starting out.'"

"Oh, I love this." I grinned. "My pots are charming and characterful. Perfect."

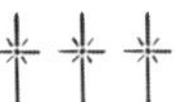

My little pots are currently in heavy rotation in my house. My blue pot holds pistachios when friends come over, and my bulgy, characterful green pot is for my morning yogurt. I'm so pleased with them.

But they're not the most gratifying results of my experiment in amateur pottery. Rather, it seems that I've fallen in love.

I'd entered into the experiment of pottery-making wondering if I had any innate talent in the craft. I think the jury is still out on this, but it doesn't matter. What I'd discovered is the *potency of curiosity*. I discovered that sitting at the wheel, in my inexperience and ineptitude, requires me to tap into something that feels a bit like courage. Rick Rubin, a record producer and the author of *The Creative Act: A Way of Being*, writes "the person who makes something today isn't the same person who returns to the work tomorrow." Unlike anything I'd tried before, pottery made me believe this statement wholeheartedly.

After that session with Bea, I ended up registering for a six-week course to go deeper into the fundamentals of wheel-throwing. I don't know if I'm ever going to go beyond creating charming pots or expert ashtrays, but that's not the point. Building the pots—and failing—pushes me to extend myself grace, and even access empathy. Over time, I've become even more curious. Because the whir of the wheel and the feel of the clay in my hands reminds me of meditation, I wondered: Are there other practices that I could try that would feel similar? Could intentional amateurism become a meditative process of self-care?

It was time to find out.

mindfulness

Mindfulness

Be Like Water, My Friend

I WAS LYING on the floor of my office, arms alongside my body, palms up, eyes closed. My webcam was on, and the computer screen was filled with images of the living spaces of about fifteen people around the world. But their inhabitants were nowhere to be seen. Instead, it was a mosaic of empty desks, sofas, kitchens. Over my speakers, a voice spoke slowly, soothingly:

> *"Begin dropping into the sensations of feeling. Breathing in . . . breathing out. Notice . . . notice this breath that you're feeling. Breathe a breath . . . nothing more . . . nothing less."*

I was two weeks into a six-week mindfulness class, and I was vaguely annoyed. *I can't believe I'm taking two hours out of my week to just lie here*, I thought. *I'm wasting time.*

The meditation lasted for forty-five minutes. At the end, Peter, the mindfulness instructor, brought us back together.

One by one, the other class participants got up from their prone positions and returned to their seats, their bleary faces reappearing on-screen.

"How did that feel?"

The class was slow to respond. I tried not to let my exasperation show. Finally, a participant named Ben spoke up.

"Today was hard for me," he said. "My mind kept drifting. But I've come to expect that now, and I just remember that there's no reason I can't begin again. In fact," he continued, "I've been reminding myself of that a lot, even outside of class. There's no reason I can't begin again at any point in my life."

"Interesting," said Peter, with a smile. I noticed that whenever we were debriefing a session, he never analyzed, agreed, or disagreed with what we said: he simply acknowledged our words, offered a few additional thoughts, and moved on. "It sounds like the difference between reacting unconsciously and responding consciously. Really interesting. Thank you for sharing. Anyone else?"

A few more people shared their opinions about the meditation, and as I listened, I calmed down a bit. I'd been frustrated that I was irritated, but it turns out I wasn't alone. For the most part, everyone described moments when their minds strayed, or even when they felt uncomfortable being in the silence for such a long time. There were one or two members of the group who had apparently achieved enlightenment in the forty-five minutes we were on the ground, but I suspected they were just giving a whole new meaning to the phrase "lying meditation."

"Thank you for sharing," said Peter again. "And thank you for participating. As I listen to you all, I'd like to simply offer this thought, from the poet Dorothy Hunt: 'Perhaps peace,' she said, 'is simply this moment without judgment.'"

Perhaps peace is simply this moment without judgment.

As I considered Peter's words, I wondered: who would I be without judgment? Judgment, and its cousin, impatience, are quite possibly my most marked negative traits and they have been since childhood. (Exhibit A: my comment about "lying meditation," above.) This was, after all, the reason I'd registered for this class. Perhaps it's the result of being the first-born child. Or maybe it's the hallmark of those who strive to be high academic achievers. Whatever the reason, what's ironic is that even before taking this class (and despite how much I'd been snapping at everyone in recent months), I would have described *patience* and *nonjudgment* as two of my most deeply held core values. I admire folks who are able to take their time with others, or breathe through frustrating moments, or show painstaking care when handling something complicated. The trick is figuring out how to cultivate these virtues in *me*.

There were four more classes to go, and thankfully, with each class I became less irritable. I found myself opening up to Peter's patient guidance as he led us through the meditation sessions. I became particularly interested in the idea that practicing mindfulness could occur not only lying in a prone position or seated in a peaceful lotus posture: Peter invited us to practice outside of the class, while we were walking or even washing dishes. All it took, it seemed, was to bring your mind to the present moment, without judgment. As Peter insisted, it was there that peace could be found, even if we weren't sitting still.

Intrigued, I decided to do a little research. Jon Kabat-Zinn was the creator of the mindfulness class I was taking, so I started by reading his works. Dr. Kabat-Zinn is a professor emeritus of medicine and the founder of the Mindfulness-Based Stress Reduction Clinic at the University of Massachusetts Medical School. He is also the author of the blockbuster best-selling book *Wherever You Go, There You Are: Mindfulness Meditation in Everyday Life*, which has sold over one million copies and remains a foundational guide to mindfulness meditation, thirty years after its publication. In his clinic, he focuses primarily on mindfulness for stress reduction, with instruction on mindfulness meditation practices based on his extensive research. Students are called to approach the courses with what he calls the "attitudes of mindfulness": nonjudging, gratitude, patience, a beginner's mind, trust, non-striving, acceptance, letting go, and generosity. According to Dr. Kabat-Zinn, working on any one of these attitudes during practice will rapidly lead you to the others. The idea, of course, is that by cultivating mindfulness during meditation, you learn how to practice mindfulness when you're *not* meditating. The course I'd been taking was focused on mindfulness during times of stress, but Peter also emphasized that it was possible to invoke mindfulness in ordinary, day-to-day life as well.

The assertion is corroborated by Dr. Ellen J. Langer, a professor of psychology at Harvard University and the author of the book *Mindfulness*. She writes: "Almost any activity can be undertaken mindfully. Being mindful allows us to be joyfully engaged in what we are doing. Time races by, and we feel fully alive."

This seemed all well and good, but as my early experience in Peter's class showed me, I was apparently gifted at practicing mindfulness while *still* feeling impatient. Given Kabat-Zinn's assertion that patience is one of the attitudes of mindfulness, I needed to figure out how to address this. So I looked up *patience,* in an attempt to figure out how to evoke it more fully. Luckily, I discovered the work of M. J. Ryan, the author of *The Power of Patience*, and her definition of the term. She writes, "A synonym of patience is self-possession. I love that word; it helps me remember that, with patience, we are in charge of our selves. We can choose how to respond to a given event, rather than being hijacked by our emotions. In this way, patience is like a keel on a boat—it allows us to keep our stability in the stormiest of seas while continuing to move in the direction we desire."

Self-possession. This felt closer to what I was looking for: a practice that would help me experiment with managing my own restlessness and, hopefully, take those skills into the rest of my life. Of all the attitudes of mindfulness, perhaps patience—self-possession—was the one I should pay most attention to. After all, as Kabat-Zinn writes, "If you cultivate patience, you almost can't help but cultivate mindfulness."

So, now that I was clearer on both mindfulness and patience and their relationship to each other, I wondered about their application in intentional amateurism. If mindfulness could be practiced while doing something else, could it be an integral part of this avocation experiment I was about to embark on? Specifically, could we reap all the benefits of mindfulness meditation simply by engaging in activities we love to do?

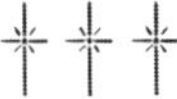

I broached the subject of mindfulness potentially being an essential part of avocational practice the next time I spoke with my friend, Alice Bradley. Alice has been an author and editor for thirty years. We've known each other for a long time, but it was ages before I discovered that in addition to her talent as a writer, she's also a gifted artist. We'd met for an early dinner one night in New York City, and she had a sketchbook with her, filled with the most enchanting sketches and watercolor paintings of her family, flora, architecture—things that had captured her attention over the years. Her talent surprised me, because at no point during our friendship had she mentioned that she's an artist.

"I was always kind of an artistic kid," she said when I asked her how long she'd been making art. "I won a few art awards, that kind of stuff. But there were definitely more talented artists around me in school, so I never thought of myself as an artist. I just liked it. Also, it's funny: I can't seem to draw from memory, so that always struck me as a good reason why I couldn't honestly call myself an artist. If you told me to draw an elephant, I would draw something unholy. I draw from images or what's in front of me."

"Well, I couldn't produce a holy drawing if you told me to draw an elephant *from* a drawing of an elephant." I grinned. "How did you get started?"

"Really, my dad." Alice's eyes became misty. It hadn't been very long since her father passed away. "My dad was an artist, and I really began to enjoy watercolor painting when it became a way for us to bond when we were together. In my thirties, I really got into it, and I took a course with him at the Brooklyn Museum of Art. It was so fun. I received a lot of encouragement from the instructors there, and the class made me want to make art more and more and more and more. I got to the point where I'd be falling asleep and thinking about watercolors, mixing paints; it was *that* kind of obsession.

"Then, about ten years ago, I did a hundred-day project where I made a watercolor every day. I shared a few on Instagram, and a few people wanted to buy them, so I thought I should sell my stuff. And I sold a couple of pieces, and suddenly . . . I didn't want to do it anymore. I just felt my love of art dying in me."

"Say more about this," I said. "Describe to me what it feels like without the pressure of selling your work."

"Well, without the pressure, I get into a flow state. I just play, making shapes. My father taught me how to do gesture drawings. We were on vacation and there was a koi pond, and he taught me how to paint the fish by just capturing the shape of the koi, the gesture, the movement—and I remember that in the process, all self-consciousness dropped away. When I'm really in the moment when I'm painting, I feel like . . . I become most *myself,* really. I feel totally present, and the critical self-narrative quiets completely. But when I paint for other people, the noise comes crashing back."

I thought back to what Peter taught me: *Peace is this moment without judgment.* "It sounds like such a mindful practice," I said.

"It absolutely is."

Unsurprisingly, there's research to support the relationship between mindfulness and what Alice described as "flow state." Dr. Kabat-Zinn defines *mindfulness* as the awareness that arises through paying attention, on purpose, in the present moment, nonjudgmentally. But *flow* is different. Coined by psychologist Mihaly Csikszentmihalyi, the term *flow* refers to the experience of an activity that is so thoroughly engrossing that there's not enough attention left over to consider either the past or the future—only the present. So while mindfulness and flow are similar—both emphasize the value of living in the moment—mindfulness can be invoked at any moment in time, while flow simply arises during pleasant experiences.

However—*and this is the supremely cool part*—mindfulness can provide the *basis* of flow and is, in fact, fertile ground for flow to appear. Alice understands this innately: She described to me how, when she sits down to create a watercolor painting, she mindfully sets the stage for encouraging flow. She has a special place in her house where she likes to paint. She lays out her favorite brushes and watercolors. She even has a playlist of music, curated exclusively for creating her art. When she's mindful in her approach to her artistic practice, flow follows. *Magic*.

"What else has mindfulness in your painting practice taught you?" I asked Alice.

She thought for a moment. "Well, it definitely helps me release control of the outcome," she replied. "You don't have a ton of control over the paint in watercolor, but you can't be tentative in watercolor, either. You have to be sort of bold and let things go where they're going to go. And that's a lesson that I've carried with me into the rest of my life, too."

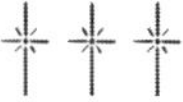

Hearing about how Alice's mindfulness in her painting practice allowed her to slip into a flow state, I wondered if there was any activity that I could begin that did the same. Then one day, I came across an article by mindfulness expert Light Watkins. He described how his relatively new swimming practice reminded him of when he was first learning the basics of meditation. With his swimming practice, the mechanics of swimming had become second nature to him, just like the mechanics of meditation had become second nature, all those years ago.

Reading this article, my next course of action became obvious:

I needed to swim.

I already knew how to swim—sort of. I'd taken obligatory lessons as a child, and I could certainly save my own life if I ever fell into the deep end of a pool. But I'd never learned to do the crawl, or even develop any cadence of breathing. So improving my swimming seemed like the perfect way to practice mindfulness. Besides, what better way to enter flow state than in the water?

For the record, if anyone who knew me well heard that I was considering doing this, they would've likely worried that I was in the throes of a neurological event. Being from the Caribbean, and therefore a card-carrying Island Girl, I have very strong feelings about the bodies of water in which I swim. I am, naturally, most comfortable in the ocean. I love the seawater on my skin, the sunshine, and the sandy beaches of my favorite places in the world. But I mostly love the ocean because of the tides and the salt. The way I figure it, if sea creatures poop in the water, the currents and tides will wash it all away from me. Plus, salt has antibacterial properties, so the number of potential waterborne bacteria that could kill me is reduced. (I realize that there are huge holes in my logic here, but just go with me on this.)

Next in line after the ocean are rivers: They don't have the benefit of antibacterial salt, but at least they have currents, so that keeps the things that could make me ill (microbes and animal poop, etc.), moving. Lakes are generally a no-go for me: no currents, no salt. Water that sits there getting dirtier and dirtier. Just no.

But pools, in my completely uneducated opinion, aren't much better. At best, they're just giant vats of diluted chlorine; at worst, they're giant vats of diluted chlorine and bodily fluids. For these reasons, only rarely in my adult life have I ever even considered entering a pool. So the fact that I was contemplating a swimming habit in a public pool—to practice *patience*, no less—was completely out of character. Still, the thought of my body sleekly cutting through the water and doing perfect kick turns was intoxicating. (Did I mention I never learned to do the crawl?)

I shared my plan with one of the most mindful, patient people I know: Joon S. Park, a chaplain at a Level 1 Trauma Center. He's also the author of *As Long as You Need*, a book about grief, self-compassion, and soul care. And as it happens, Joon is a sixth-degree black belt in Tae Kwon Do.

"I'm about to embark on a swimming practice as a vehicle for practicing mindfulness, and I imagine that mindfulness is a big part of your work." I said.

"It is," he said. "We're assigned maybe thirty to fifty consults each day. So naturally, sometimes I want to rush a visit, so that I can tick that consult off the list. That's very honest and human. But if I'm to do my job correctly, I have to forget the numbers, the stream of activity around me, the checklist. Instead, I need to be with my patient, who is having the hardest day of her life in this moment. That takes an intentional choice. It takes being very present in my body.

"So, while I sanitize before I enter every single room, I pray a very simple prayer: 'God, how do you want to work through me?' It's very open-ended, because I want to remind myself to be open to whatever the patient tells me: to their story, to their emotions. If they're angry, if they're going to lash out, if they're numb and don't want to talk, or they try to kick me out of the room, I'm open to all of it.

"In other words, mindfulness, to me, is almost like a learned language. It doesn't always come naturally to us. But we can all do it, because it takes just one simple thing: a pause. The pause can get us from judgment to grace. It takes us from shame to grace."

Perhaps peace is simply this moment without judgment.

"Did you learn this in your Tae Kwon Do practice?" I asked. "Is mindfulness part of your life as an athlete?"

"Well, I retired about ten years ago, but I grew up in the dojo. And yes, there's something so centering and healing and releasing about any kind of exercise. When we connect with our bodies, something chemical and spiritual happens. Exercise is a way of being patient and caring with ourselves and loving our bodies. In fact, I've often thought that what I did as a martial arts instructor, building bodily and physical confidence with my students through mindful practice, is similar to what I do as a chaplain, helping the bereaved attain more grief literacy. It's about my practicing mindfulness and being open to understanding how each student or patient has different ideas of what it means to throw a 'perfect' punch or be 'perfect' in navigating their grief, and then helping them to practice their own patience with themselves, knowing that each person will have an individual experience that ultimately works for them."

I decided that I wouldn't tell Joon that I'd now officially adopted him as my de facto swim coach, lest he decline the honor. Instead, I admitted that I fully expected to be awful at my new swimming practice. "Do you have any advice for how I should approach this?" I asked.

Joon grinned. "I'm thinking of that old Bruce Lee saying, 'Be like water, my friend.' Water can fit into a cup, it can flow, it can crash. I think there's something very beautiful about giving up your sense of control or expectation or outcome. In fact, I think there's *grief* in that. So my advice would be when you jump in the water, perhaps you surrender to the water just a bit. Like the prayer I say when I see my patients that helps me be open to them, maybe you say something like asking the water, 'What do you want to do today?' Befriend the water. Just give yourself to the water and to the moment. Be open."

The decision made and advice received, I promptly did the next obvious thing: I began putting off going to the pool. For months. I came up with every possible reason why a swimming practice was a bad idea, over and above the vat-of-questionable-liquids thing. I worried that the water would be too cold. I worried that the chlorine would turn my hair green. I worried that small children would point and laugh. The list was endless, to the point that my procrastination was so intense, the mere idea of going to the pool at all started to feel shameful.

And then my daughter, Alex, returned home from college for spring break. No sooner had she dropped her bags in our hallway than she announced to Marcus and me that she planned to go swimming every day during her week off. Alex had been hired on staff at a large summer camp in east Texas. "Everyone has to take a swimming test so we can save the campers if needed," she said. "I need to start moving to make sure I pass." Although Alex is a strong swimmer, Marcus (a stellar swimmer himself) offered to help her, and they made a plan to go to the gym pool.

It appeared my time had arrived.

We arrived at the gym and discovered there were actually *two* pools available to us: a long one, with cooler water, and a shorter one, with warm. Guess which one I chose.

The pool was sparkling clear, and given the pungent odor of chlorine that hung in the air, it was obvious that the staff took cleanliness very seriously. (*Thank God.*) Marcus and Alex wasted no time claiming a lane and immediately began to swim. I picked a lane far from the two of them, because I love them and there was no need for them to witness the spectacle that I was about to make. I kicked off my slides, dropped my towel, and slipped into the water. As advertised, it was pleasantly warm.

I took a deep breath, and remembered how Alice mindfully set the stage to make her art. I remembered Joon's words. *What do you want to do today, water?* I thought to myself.

And then I surrendered and started making my way across the pool.

I'm not sure how to describe my swimming technique except by using animal metaphors. For example, Marcus is clearly a dolphin: He cuts through the water sleekly, as if he has suddenly grown a fin. Alex is similar, but she's more of an otter: fast and playful, slicing through any body of water with ease. In other words, they're both positively aquadynamic. I am not like them. I don't doggy paddle, exactly, because my movements aren't that frantic. I am more of a turtle: comfortable in the water but slow, and I don't look particularly elegant when I swim.

So I began "turtling" across the pool. I hadn't brought goggles, my first mistake, and I realized that I didn't want to open my eyes underwater, lest they burn from the chlorine (and—*shudder*—any other fluids). By the time I'd turtled to the opposite end, keeping my head above water, I was completely out of breath. But I was determined, so I turtled my way back again.

Marcus caught my eye, and he looked alarmed. "Are you okay?" he mouthed. I nodded, gasping.

That evening I was only able to do sixteen lengths—eight laps—and it took hours before my heart rate returned to normal. But a few days later, when I returned to the pool, Marcus let me borrow his goggles, and they made a world of difference. Without worrying about seeing or my eyes burning, I was able to relax into the strokes. I reminded myself that my goal wasn't speed; it was patience. And I became more mindful, noticing the way my body and my mind reacted to the warm water as I swam. I noticed the bubbles as I exhaled, and I sensed the calming of my mind.

So began my swimming practice: Every other day, I returned to the pool. I bought my own goggles and wore a favorite swimsuit, effectively setting the stage to help maximize flow. Before each session, I took a deep breath and entered the water with a mindful intention of being open to the experience. I noted how I felt in the water, without judgment, simply witnessing how it might have differed from the previous day's swim. Over time, I relaxed into my practice: I learned how to breathe in the water without getting winded. I noticed which muscles felt sore, and which felt stronger. I quickly worked my way up to twenty-five laps—fifty lengths!—and while I was still turtling, I was doing it with more cadence.

Through this openness, I discovered that, like for Alice, self-criticism would fall away. I'd notice the thrill of kicking off at each end of the pool, and the way the bubbles would rush past my ears as I exhaled. I would focus on the dark line of the pool lane, and surprise myself with ideas for my writing and other aspects of my creative work that would occasionally pop into my head. And after a time, I realized with some shock that my swimming practice actually *did* inspire flow.

A few months after that first night I entered the pool with Marcus and Alex, I realized that if I skipped my regular swim practice, I missed it. Once the focus of my practice had shifted to mindfulness—to the *experience* of each session—rather than how much chlorine was in the pool or mastering the crawl, swimming became, well, meditative, almost a spiritual practice. And that is absolutely worth spending my time in a vat of questionable fluids.

I can't say that I've noticed that I'm more patient in real life as yet, but I do know that I like myself when I'm turtling across the pool. Also, I'm kinder to myself. Like Alice, I've learned how to release control: I've become less concerned about the fact that I don't do a perfect freestyle stroke and am instead surrendering to my own swimming cadence. I'm no Katie Ledecky, but I'm definitely delighting in the process. Could this be . . . self-compassion? Was there another avocation I could attempt—or one that I'd done earlier in life that I could return to—that would inspire this grace as part of my intentional amateurism experiment?

I returned to my menu to see.

self-compassion

Self-Compassion

We're Not Beethoven

A SIX-TIME GRAMMY award winner, Billy Joel is one of the world's best-selling singer-songwriters. Born in the Bronx in New York City, Joel was enrolled in piano lessons at age four. By high school, he was playing in piano bars to help his family make ends meet. Because of his work schedule, he ended up missing a crucial English test that prevented him from graduating, but he remained undaunted: "To hell with it," he declared. "If I'm not going to Columbia University, I'm going to Columbia Records, and you don't need a high school diploma there."

Turns out this was a stellar decision. "Piano Man"—the title track of Joel's debut album—was his first Top 20 single, and the album was his first gold album. His album *An Innocent Man* had six Top 40 singles, and he's had thirty-three Top 40 hits in all. He is the recipient of the Grammy Legend Award and is a Kennedy Center honoree. He has been inducted into the Rock & Roll Hall of Fame, the Madison Square Garden Hall of Fame, the Hollywood

Walk of Fame, and the Long Island Music and Entertainment Hall of Fame.

Impressive, right? And yet, after releasing his 1993 album *River of Dreams*, Billy Joel stopped composing songs.

In a 2018 interview, when asked why he no longer pursued songwriting, his response was surprising. "I couldn't be as good as I wanted to," he said. "It was driving me crazy. It was wrecking my personal life, too, just not being able to be satisfied. And drinking became a problem because of that, to try to drown my frustration with it."

He continued: "There's a quote from Neil Diamond. He said, 'I've forgiven myself for not being Beethoven.' And I read that quote, and I said, '*That's* my problem. I have not forgiven myself for not being Beethoven.' And I still, to this day, haven't."

Perfectionism is a hell of a thing, ain't it?

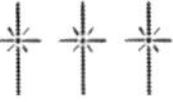

Perfectionism is the compulsive need to achieve and accomplish goals, with no allowance or grace for falling short. It can become crippling: Not only does perfectionism keep iconic musical artists from creating, it can keep the rest of us from even *trying*. What's worse, unchecked perfectionism affects our health, resulting in heightened stress levels, burnout, anxiety, workaholism, even depression. Researcher and author Dr. Brené Brown closely ties perfectionism to low self-worth, maintaining that at its core, perfectionism is about attempting to earn the approval of others. "Healthy striving is self-focused: how can I improve?" she writes. "Perfectionism is other-focused: what will they think? Perfectionism is a hustle."

Those of us who struggle with perfectionism often find it terrifying to attempt anything new—or even to simply pursue what we love. We worry about disappointing ourselves, or that we might look foolish to others. And honestly, hustling to meet the impossible standards of what "they" will think is downright exhausting.

But *not* doing what we love, or avoiding trying something new, inevitably precludes us from learning, adventure, and even joy. So how do we combat perfectionism, especially in pursuing intentional amateurism?

Enter self-compassion.

Self-compassion is the antidote to perfectionism. When we practice self-compassion, we cultivate emotional resilience, motivation, and growth. Dr. Kristin Neff, professor at the University of Texas and author of the book *Self-Compassion: The Proven Power of Being Kind to Yourself*, has found that self-compassion is an even more powerful deterrent to perfectionism than high self-esteem. According to Neff, research shows that that since high self-esteem often inherently involves ranking ourselves against others, when people try to maintain that sense of elevated self-esteem, they fall into traps like narcissism, self-absorption, self-righteous anger, prejudice, discrimination, and more.

Self-compassion, on the other hand, is the perfect alternative to self-esteem. “It offers the same protection against harsh self-criticism as self-esteem, but without the need to see ourselves as better than others,” Neff writes. “In other words, self-compassion provides the same benefits as high self-esteem, without its drawbacks.”

There’s a further benefit: practicing self-compassion may trigger the production of oxytocin. This amazing hormone reduces fear and anxiety and counteracts the increased blood pressure and cortisol associated with stress. Better still, research indicates that increased levels of oxytocin amplify feelings of trust, calm, safety, generosity, and connectedness.

And who doesn’t need more of *that* in their life, I ask you?

During a recent conversation I had with a friend, she testified to the powerful therapeutic effect of self-compassion. But what’s amazing is that she experienced its healing powers in an unlikely place: the roller-skating rink.

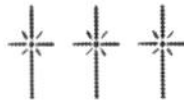

Denise Phillips Wade is a schoolteacher, singer, breast cancer survivor, and an avid roller-skater. It all began in a suburb of Houston, on a street that bore her last name.

“I used to roller-skate all the time,” she told me. “I began skating when I was ten years old. It was my daily activity. The road in front of our house was on land my dad owned and was named after him: Phillips Lane. So I had free rein of about a mile of pavement. And then, when I was thirteen or fourteen, I started going to the local rink."

I asked Denise why she loved roller-skating so much, and her answer was simple: It was *fun*. "I loved the *music*, and, also, I loved doing all the tricks—sticking one leg out and skating on the other, bent leg—all of it. I was even part of a group of friends who skated together, and we would all dress alike. We'd decorate our knee socks with pom-poms, and our skates with them as well, so it looked like we were wearing pom-pom skate boots." She laughed at the memory.

"Amazing," I said. "You did this all through high school?"

"Yes! But when I went to university, there weren't any rinks nearby, so I stopped skating."

"Why did you eventually return?"

"Because of my breast cancer journey." Here, Denise grew sober. "Luckily, the doctors caught the cancer early, but because my father had breast cancer, I opted for a double mastectomy. It was a ten-and-a-half-hour surgery. They removed my lymph nodes to test them, and they were fine, so I didn't have to do chemo or radiation."

"Well, thank heavens for small mercies. How long was recovery?"

"The actual recovery was about six months, but in many ways, I'm still recovering. That's why skating has been so helpful: It's a way to choose the positive. We live in a world of opposites, and we always have the opportunity to choose how we respond to challenges. I always try to choose a positive approach."

"I love this philosophy," I said. "But choosing to return to roller-skating after a ten-and-a-half-hour surgery, with six months of recovery, and decades away from the sport couldn't have been easy."

Denise smiled. "It wasn't. But skating has always felt like flying to me, and I wanted to release those good endorphins."

"So how did you go about it? Did you just drive to the rink one day and see how you did?"

"Well, first, a year after the surgery, I talked to my doctor about returning. Recovery had required that I remain lying down and still for so long that I'd experienced severe muscle atrophy, mostly in my thighs. I suggested to my doctor that roller-skating might be a good way for me to regain my strength. He agreed and cleared me.

"Of course, returning to the rink was really difficult, because my body had changed so much. I could feel it. I didn't have the strength. I had the muscle memory but not the muscles. So I was terrified, because I was so unstable. I just took it really, really easy on myself the first time. I asked myself, 'Can I make it around the rink just five times?' But man, just going around the rink one time and feeling the breeze on me—it just made me keep wanting to return to the rink and try harder."

I was fascinated by Denise's description of returning to a thing you loved a long time ago and rediscovering the sheer joy of doing it. Eventually I decided to ask her the question I couldn't get out of my head. "What's your end game?" I asked. "I mean, are you trying to get as good as you were when you were a teenager?"

Denise was quiet for a moment. "Nowadays, I go to the rink every Tuesday and Thursday, for about two-and-a-half hours at a time," she said. "And I think my goal might be twofold, and it might be layered. My initial goal was simply to get stronger, but I'm not talking about just physically stronger. When you're battling cancer, you feel weak in all areas—physically, but also mentally, and emotionally, and even spiritually weak. So roller-skating is sort of a starting point for me to gain strength in all of those areas. Then secondly, I'm hoping that by becoming stronger, I'll build confidence in all other areas of my life—like in combatting stage fright when I sing, for example. I want to be able to think to myself, *hey, I accomplished this, so I'm going to take this greatness and pour it into the next thing I want to achieve.*"

Herein lies the brilliance of Denise's roller-skating practice: not that her avocation is an exercise in achieving mastery, but that she *shifted her definition of what it means to be good at it.* Rather than setting an idealistic goal of skating-queen perfection, or even recapturing the slick moves of her youth, Denise is showing her changing and evolving body compassion. She consulted her doctor about her current capacities and limitations. She gently coaxed her body into pleasurable movement. She delighted in the time at the rink—the breeze as she made her circles around the perimeter, the beats of her favorite music. Ultimately, her commitment to self-compassion, mindful pleasure, and intentional amateurism brings her the gifts of joy and confidence.

And I bet those gifts feel a hell of a lot more rewarding than the ability to stick one leg out and skate on the other, bent leg.

After speaking with Denise, I couldn't help but feel a pang of envy. Like her, I used to do many things as a kid that I'd love to do now. And while I might say "I'm too busy" or even "I've moved on" to explain away the reason I haven't returned to doing them, the truth is that self-compassion isn't as easy as it sounds. Dusting off those roller skates, or grabbing the violin from the attic, or reaching for those oil paints after a long hiatus, especially when your moves don't come as easily as they used to: These things are *hard*. Why would I do something I used to do when I know I'll never be as good at it as I was when I was young? How will I keep from sinking into embarrassment, or worse yet, shame?

Luckily, there's a way. According to Dr. Neff, there are three elements of self-compassion. The first is *mindfulness*, which Dr. Neff describes as "the clear seeing and nonjudgmental acceptance of what's occurring in the present moment." In other words, mindfulness is about stopping and acknowledging a situation as it is, without assigning a value, positive or negative. Denise did this when she acknowledged her muscle atrophy, consulted with her doctor to determine the exact extent to which she was impaired, and did what was necessary to get his go-ahead to attempt skating again. This wasn't about lamenting her illness. This was about establishing and acknowledging her body's starting point.

The second element of self-compassion, according to Dr. Neff, is a recognition of our *common humanity,* defined as "a feeling of connectedness with others in the experience of life, rather than feeling isolated and alienated in our suffering." This element is about recognizing that our feelings of challenge, grief, or loss are normal, that anyone in a similar situation would feel exactly the same way. Again, Denise illustrated this element beautifully when she acknowledged how battling cancer affects everyone—not just physically, but emotionally and spiritually—and therefore her struggles and challenges were perfectly natural and part of the human condition.

The final element of self-compassion is *self-kindness*, which Dr. Neff describes as being "gentle and understanding with ourselves, rather than harshly critical or judgmental." Again, Denise demonstrated this when she limited herself to only circling the rink five times and leaned into the way the breeze felt as she skated. And by continuing to be gentle with herself, she began regaining her strength while sustaining her joy.

The beauty of understanding these three elements, according to Dr. Neff, is that when we do start to feel overwhelmed or overcome by embarrassment, shame, or despair, we can give ourselves "self-compassion breaks," during which we recall these three elements before proceeding further. Here's how these breaks work:

When we're feeling dismay or overwhelm—no matter how big or small the emotion—we first take a moment to acknowledge the feeling. We do this by saying to ourselves, "This is hard" or "I'm feeling really discouraged right now." This is the *mindfulness* part of the self-compassion break: acknowledging that we're in a difficult moment.

The second step is to recognize that it's normal to feel how we feel. We take a moment to say to ourselves, "We all struggle at some point in our lives," or "Anyone in my situation would feel exactly as I do," while placing our hands over our hearts. This practice invokes the *common humanity* element of self-compassion and is a reminder that we are not alone and that our feelings are completely natural.

The final step is to say affirming, encouraging words like, "May I be kind to myself." This step invokes—you guessed it—the *self-kindness* element of self-compassion. This increases those feelings of calm, trust, and safety that can help us proceed.

The self-compassion breaks we give ourselves might only last for thirty seconds or so. But when done intentionally, such a break can be all we need to ground us enough to practice intentional amateurship with the same meaning, purpose, and joy that Denise does when she roller-skates. And I don't know about you, but I can always use more meaning, purposes, joy and self-compassion in my life.

It was time to put this into practice.

My mother grew up playing piano beautifully, and she was insistent: All young women should learn to play an instrument, and that included me. So when I was seven or so, living in that fishing village in Trinidad, my mother began searching for someone who could teach me how to play. As it happened, one of the American expats who lived in our village, Mrs. Deerhake, was a gifted pianist, and she was open to giving lessons to the local children. Mom eagerly enrolled me as one of Mrs. Deerhake's first students.

When I began my tutelage with Mrs. Deerhake, my legs weren't even long enough to reach the pedals of the piano. But this wasn't a problem; pedals, I learned, were for *advanced* piano. I first needed to learn where middle C was located, and what an octave was. Mrs. Deerhake was a patient teacher, pointing out the major and minor scales, which I dutifully practiced. Every year, Mrs. Deerhake would hold small recitals during which the other students and I, dressed in our Sunday best, would gather in her living room and bang out classics like "Three Blind Mice" or "London Bridge Is Falling Down," while our parents sat smiling through gritted teeth.

Eventually, my family moved to the United States, where I continued taking lessons for several years—now

I was even able to reach the pedals!—but after a while, I grew bored with the classical pieces my instructors insisted on teaching me. So to my mother's chagrin, I quit. But I always had a good ear, and for many more years I continued teaching myself piano. I was never a great pianist, but I was a decent one. And I kept playing until I graduated from university and officially moved out of my parents' house and away from their piano.

Years passed.

When I spoke with Denise about her return to roller-skating, I wondered if there was something from my past that might be worth returning to, and I remembered the piano. Marcus had bought himself a keyboard a few years earlier, and it was just sitting upstairs, collecting dust. Maybe it was time to dust it off and give it a go?

The more I considered it, the more excited I got—but also, weirdly, the more I hesitated. It had been so long since I sat in front of a keyboard that I was afraid of how I would sound. Would I remember how to read the music? Would my playing sound fluid? Would I remember where middle C was?

Would I make an ass of myself?

After a few weeks, I got tired of stalling and decided the day had come to push myself. Initially, I thought I'd attempt Bach's Prelude in C Major: It was a piece that I used to play, and I'd always enjoyed Bach's melodies. But then I remember how much I grew bored by learning classical music. And besides, what I really wanted to do was try something completely new—maybe a more modern piece would hold my attention.

So I scrolled through my playlist on Spotify, looking for music that I would be excited to play. It took a minute, but I found one: "Best Part," by singer-songwriter Daniel Caesar. The arrangement that I found was in D major (which meant the challenge of remembering to play two sharps), and there was even a section where I'd have to cross my left hand over my right to play a chord. That felt *fancy*. I purchased and downloaded the sheet music to my tablet and headed to the keyboard.

I decided that before I even attempted the piece, I should limber up. After all, that's what Mrs. Deerhake would've had me do. I found middle C (*success!*) and began slowly playing the D major scale.

And I was *awful*.

My fingers had a mind of their own. Sometimes I'd will a finger to move and it would just lie there stiffly on the keys; other times my fingers would rapidly play notes in succession even though I was trying to play at a deliberate cadence. Although I was alone, I felt a sudden flush of embarrassment. Maybe even shame.

I stopped playing.

This is hard, I thought. And suddenly, the three steps of the self-compassion break came rushing to mind. *What was the first, again? Oh, right, mindfulness.* I allowed myself to notice the embarrassment I was feeling. Then I thought of the second element: common humanity. *Of course this is hard,* I thought. *It has been literally decades since I sat at a keyboard. This would be challenging for anyone who had been away from the piano for this long.*

I inhaled deeply and exhaled slowly. Time for the third element. "May I be kind to myself," I whispered, and returned my hands to the keyboard.

There was no denying I felt calmer. I began playing the scale again, slowly, over and over. When my fingers felt warmed up, I looked at the sheet music. And I played the first chord, and then the next.

I wasn't good, by anyone's measure. But I was surprised at how easily my fingers found the keys, without having to stop and look for them. I knew instinctively how long to hold a quarter note as opposed to an eighth note. And even the musical notations felt familiar.

Hello, old friend.

Before I knew it, an hour had passed. I've since returned to the keyboard, about every other day, and gradually the melodies and harmonies of "Best Part" began to emerge. I was tired—trying to remember everything I'd learned on the piano decades earlier was exhausting, it turns out—but I was pleased. I was calm. And I even felt proud of myself!

I had asked Denise what returning to the rink had taught her about herself. Her answer had been thoughtful. "This might sound sort of corny, but it's taught me about grit and greatness," she said. "When I was in the middle of recovering cancer, it was easy to ask all these questions, like, *Oh my goodness, why me? I don't drink, I don't smoke, I don't do anything unhealthy, why would I get this?* But the truth is that any great person we ever witness didn't achieve greatness without their own trials and tribulations—we just never saw what those challenges were."

After dealing with the cancer, she told me, "Skating feels like one small step toward *my own* idea of greatness, for *myself.* Twice a week, I wear earbuds and listen to my favorite music, and I'm able to discharge all the negatives I've ever experienced in the rink. I do that by showing up and being consistent—that's *grit.* Skating teaches me what I must do in the rest of my life, outside of the rink."

This made complete sense.

As for me, I'll never have the virtuosity of, say, Billy Joel. But I've learned that it takes grit to return to something I used to do well. It requires showing myself compassion by releasing the idea of perfection I'd held in my youth and embracing the evolution of my current capabilities.

I'm loving the practice, and I love how the sounds of the keyboard return me to my adolescence, with all the good and bad and awkwardness and promise that time of life entailed.

But most of all, I love how the piano returns me to joy. And that is more music than I could have ever hoped to make.

play

Play

Lessons from a Toilet-Roll Mermaid

I AM THE daughter of a Trinidadian engineer and a schoolteacher, and in our house academic success was valued above all else. I didn't play sports, and art was something to appreciate, not create. The only extracurricular activity I was involved with that met with my parents' approving smiles, and not raised eyebrows, was the math club. (No, I wasn't popular in high school; why do you ask?)

I followed in my father's footsteps and studied engineering at university; however, because I am a rebel, instead of pursuing petroleum engineering as he had, I enrolled in the civil engineering department. Four years later, I crossed the stage with my bachelor's degree and went out into the world, ready to engineer my tail off.

I lasted two years.

I found engineering work impossibly rigid. Day after day, I did the same work, calculating the same formulas for virtually identical structures: pipe racks at oil refineries. And as a baby engineer with a mere bachelor's degree, I quickly learned that the last thing anyone expected me to do was experiment. This was for a good reason. When you're a civil engineer—especially if you're not a researcher or an academic—you must calculate the *absolutely correct* answer. Otherwise, the building falls down, the dam crumbles, the refinery explodes. In other words, *people die*. There's no "let's see what happens if . . ."

So by the time I'd left engineering, the desire to experiment—far less, to *play*—had been driven out of me, both at work and in life. It turns out that despite my career choice, my experience isn't uncommon. At least that's what the research of Dr. Stuart Brown indicates.

A psychiatrist and the founder of the National Institute for Play, Dr. Brown has dedicated his entire career to studying human play. In his seminal book, *Play: How It Shapes the Brain, Opens the Imagination and Invigorates the Soul*, Dr. Brown describes how, over time, we tend to forget about play. "At some point as we get older . . . we are made to feel guilty for playing," he writes. "We are told that it is unproductive, a waste of time, even sinful. . . . We strive to always be productive, and if an activity doesn't teach us a skill, make us money, or get on the boss's good side, then we feel we should not be doing it. Sometimes the sheer demands of daily living seem to rob us of the ability to play." As if our busy schedules aren't enough, Dr. Brown further contends that because we internalize these messages, we end up actually shaming ourselves into giving up play.

Boy, *that* felt familiar.

Yet far into adulthood, play remains good for us. Research indicates that play activity helps to sculpt the brain, allowing us to make new cognitive connections that find their way into our everyday lives. It helps make us—and our worlds—new again; it's not called "re-creation" for nothing. And finally, play is what makes life manageable: "The opposite of play is not work," says Dr. Brown; "the opposite of play is depression."

Although I wasn't depressed, it had been a while since I'd done anything that could be called "play," and I wasn't sure I remembered how to do it. So I turned to my friend Jeff Harry. Jeff is a leadership consultant and global play expert who helps teams to build psychological safety and individuals to address their biggest challenges, all through play. He has spoken at conferences and Fortune 500 companies around the world, so I knew he would be the perfect person to help me parse play, experimentation, and challenge.

"Jeff, I've always thought of play as something . . . I don't know, *superficial*," I began. "Frivolous, even."

"Oh, but it's not!" Jeff was emphatic. "Play is a joyful act, in which you're fully immersed in the moment, and you are fully you. You know you're at play when you are so fully present that nothing else matters. Play is built from curiosity, a sense of wonder, and a sense of awe, not the constant attempt to be right. When you're in play, you're in flow."

"Okay, that sounds great, but I'm not sure I fully understand the 'constant attempt to be right' part," I said. "You say that play is a joyful act where you forget about time, right? Well, I recently started learning pottery-making, and by your definition, making pottery, for me, is play. It's definitely an act in which I experience joy, and I lose track of time."

"Beautiful," said Jeff.

"But I'm *obsessed* with getting better at it," I continued. "I watch Instagram and YouTube videos constantly to learn different methods, and then I can't wait to get back to the studio to try them out. Once I've gotten something down, I'm eager to learn the next technique. Isn't that about perfection and getting things right?"

"Well, let's examine that," he said. "When you're trying to improve, who are you doing that for?"

"I mean . . . me. Who else would I be doing it for?"

"That's *exactly* my point." Jeff grinned. "When we talk about 'perfectionism' or constantly attempting to be right, we're concerned about what *other* people think of our performance. What I hear you describing is about being curious about your own abilities. About enjoying experimentation. Your goal isn't about the end result so much as it is an inquiry into your activity and your reaction to it. It's about disconnecting yourself from the quality of your results as defined by other people. And to an extent, it's also about disconnecting yourself from *your own expectations of yourself*."

"Whoa." I exhaled. He had put precise words to my experience.

"*Yeah.*" Jeff remained quiet as he watched me consider what he'd said.

"So play can *include* challenge and experimentation," I said slowly, trying to find the right way to express the question that I was wrestling with. "And play requires an experimentation mindset?"

"Exactly. Experimentation *is* play. There's no right answer. Experimentation just gives you more data to get curious about. Of course, curiosity can be challenging. But with a mindset of experimentation, judgment falls away and you get lost in your play."

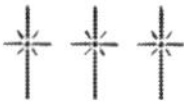

It took some time to wrap my mind around Jeff's words. Whenever I've heard the word *play*, I think of kids at a playground: on a swing set, maybe, or a merry-go-round. But it turns out that play is much broader than this. According to Dr. Stuart Brown, there are seven properties of play:

The first is *apparent purposelessness*: There's no real reason for play, it doesn't earn the player money or put food on the player's table. Play is simply play for play's sake. We play . . . just to play.

Second, play is *voluntary*. Play isn't obligatory or done out of a sense of duty. Nobody makes you play; you just want to play.

Third, play is *fun*. Play makes you feel good and usually cures boredom. Play brings you happiness.

Fourth, when we play, we *lose sense of time*. And fifth, we experience a *diminished consciousness of self*. (Interestingly, these fourth and fifth elements are hallmarks of *flow*, which we discussed in Chapter 4.)

Sixth, play has *improvisational potential*. When we play, we're open to serendipity, chance, and experimentation. We play to see what happens next.

And finally, play provides what Dr. Brown calls *continuation desire*: We don't want the fun to end.

When we consider these seven properties, it's easy to see why play is an integral part of intentional amateurism. "When we get play right, all other areas of our life go better," Dr. Brown writes. "When we ignore play, we start to have problems." Intentional amateurism provides us with a way to ensure that we make play an important focus of our lives—and therefore, our overall well-being is brighter.

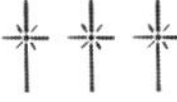

No one immerses herself in the concepts of challenge, experimentation, and play more than Marsha Shandur. A former radio presenter and DJ for Xfm Radio in the United Kingdom, Marsha is now a communications consultant who helps organizations and people create connections through storytelling. In her time off, however, she is a keen maker of automata.

I met Marsha—or rather, was introduced to her infectious enthusiasm—when she responded to an article I'd written teasing the subject matter of this book. She was the first person who responded to the article, and her comment was full of exclamation points and capital letters: It was clear that she was *overflowing* with excitement about her intentional amateurism practice. "Oh I have been thinking about this topic a TON," she gushed, "because last year I started a HOBBY. I absolutely love—and *so much* of my pleasure is derived from—how much of an amateur I am at it!!"

Needless to say, I was compelled to reach out to her to find out more. I emailed her directly, and her animated response told me her hobby was in *automata*, a word I'd never heard of and vaguely wondered if she'd made up. So we set up a time to meet via videoconference, so she could tell me all about it.

"What in heaven's name is an automata?" I asked on the afternoon when we finally connected.

"Automaton," she corrected, pronouncing the word aw-TOM-ah-ton. "*Automata* is plural. An automaton is a little machine that, when you turn a handle, does a thing—and doesn't need electricity to do it. Actually, technically, they don't have to be little. Grandfather clocks and gramophones are automata, for example. But I only make little ones."

"How did you get into making automata?" I said the unfamiliar word slowly, trying to put the accent on the correct syllables as she had.

"Well, I've always enjoyed making art as a kid, but I didn't have any natural skills at it, so I dropped it. But when I was a tween, there was a museum in Covent Garden in

London called the Cabaret Mechanical Theatre. It was full of automata. And the stuff they had—oh my goodness, it was incredible. There was one that depicted a dream: A girl sits up in bed, and then she lies back down and goes to sleep, then a giant snake appears out of a closet and goes back in, and then she sits back up again, and then a horse goes past a window and looks in . . . all by turning one small crank. Mesmerizing!"

Marsha continued, her face flushed with excitement. "I've always followed the progress of the museum, and a few years ago they began doing online courses. So one January, I signed up for their six-week course. I was the only non-artist in the class. The museum sent a kit to the homes of everyone who was enrolled, and for the first hour of each class, they would do an online studio tour with a professional automata artist. Then the second hour, we would go into virtual breakout rooms and tinker with our kits."

It sounded like a lot of fun to me, and I asked her to show me something she made. Marsha got up and left the room, returning a minute later with a small object in her hand. "My daughter is my art director. The movie *The Little Mermaid* was just about to be released, so she requested a mermaid."

Marsha began turning a tiny handle, and the small contraption in her hand sprang to life. "So here she is," she said. On my computer screen, I could make out a tiny hand-drawn mermaid, colored with crayon. "She's made out of a toilet roll and a bit of card. When she's properly aligned, she dances from side to side, and the fish swim around her. Can you see that?"

"I can!" I was delighted. "And she's so small!"

"Well, I like making really tiny things because they're cute, but also because they're so complicated. Like, sometimes I don't have enough room to maneuver a cam or get enough purchase. Making an automaton is just a series of creating problems for myself and then figuring out how to fix them. And there's such a sense of achievement when I figure it out for myself. I get so engaged, I can't think of anything else."

"It sounds like you're fully hooked," I said.

"I am." Marsha grinned. "To make sure I kept at it after I took the course, I invited my classmates, who are located around the globe, to meet on Zoom with me once a month for two hours. I cannot stress enough how talented everyone else in my automata club is: They carve wood, paint beautifully, and come up with complex contraptions that I never could. Meanwhile, I'm mostly stringing together bits of wire with garbage I find in my house. But weirdly, this doesn't make me feel in any way inadequate—only delighted. Making automata is my most favorite way to play."

The way that Marsha has embraced this new little avocation, which she described as creating problems for herself and then figuring out how to fix them, was really inspiring. Was there anything that I could do to inspire the same sort of challenge, while also being fun? Was there something I could do to actually *play*?

There was.

When I first began photography, in a time before digital cameras and camera phones, learning required purchasing a lot of film. *A lot*. I tried different brands of color film, like Kodachrome and Fuji, to learn which produced the vibrant images I liked, and many different black-and-white films before finally setting on Ilford. I asked questions—*so* many questions—of every competent photographer I knew. I took copious notes about my camera settings as I shot, and I noted how they affected the final developed prints. And once digital photography and Photoshop came along? Well, I was off and running. The immediate ability to see what I'd shot, coupled with the ability to process my own photos, was a game changer. Suddenly, my daily practice was paying off in spades. I created my own style, and was proud when someone told me that my work was recognizable and distinctive.

After decades of near daily shooting, however, my practice had become rote. It's not that I didn't love photography anymore; making images remains one of my favorite pastimes. But I was no longer *challenged*. I know my way around a camera, I'm comfortable processing images (and can now do so in minutes instead of hours), but I definitely wasn't continuously learning anymore. It didn't feel like *play*.

So one day, I wondered: *How can I make creating imagery more of a challenge?* And it came to me: I could learn to make video.

Here's where I admit that I chose filmmaking because I believed it would be a bit of a challenge, but not *too* much of one. After all, I have thirty years' experience framing shots! Understanding f-stops! Fiddling with contrast! Sharpness! Saturation! Surely this knowledge would give me a substantial leg up on learning filmmaking. I thought I'd be rivaling the Coppola family in absolutely no time.

Ha! Ha, ha, ha, ha . . . ha. It turns out video is *hard.*

I began by grabbing my old DSLR camera, and for the first time, turning on the video setting. *I'll just take a short video of what it looks like to make a mug of tea*, I thought. *Two minutes tops.* I put the kettle on and began shooting.

As soon as I aimed the camera, it was clear that I had absolutely no idea what I was doing. Maintaining focus was impossible. Figuring out how to move the camera in interesting ways was confounding. And after I uploaded what I'd shot into the free video-editing software that came with my laptop, I was horrified. The footage was so shaky that it looked like I'd turned on the camera while in the throes of a seizure. Despite all my efforts in processing, the final result looked flat, as compared to the warmth I was able to elicit from my photographs.

Realizing that this was going to be far more challenging than I'd anticipated, I became more determined. First of all, I needed to ensure that I had the right tools. Marcus (aka,

Tech Support) helped me figure out what kind of equipment I needed. (Answer: A gimbal that removes camera shake was clearly at the top of the list.) My own research confirmed that as a beginner, my free video-editing software was more than enough.

Next, I began a deep exploration of the work of talented filmmakers. I collected videos like some people collect stamps. I looked for hobbyists who make vivid, action-packed imagery, and I searched for "slow life" influencers, folks who created dreamy scenes of cozy homes and gardens filmed at golden hour, casting halos around flowers covered in flitting butterflies and buzzy bees. I combed through the work of commercial videographers and studied their lighting techniques and shooting angles. I watched feature films by prominent filmmakers—Spike Lee, Wes Anderson, Sophia Coppola—and took note of what I loved about their work. In each case, I kept meticulous records of the approaches I wanted to try.

Finally, I contacted a group of friends—people who I hoped wouldn't mind receiving my decidedly amateur films—and asked if they'd be open to being my test audience. I didn't ask for their feedback (not that I wouldn't have gratefully accepted it); honestly, their feedback wasn't that important to me. I was more interested in simply having them keep me accountable. I figured that if a group of people was expecting to receive my videos, I darn well had better make them.

And then I got to work.

After experimenting with camera filters, scriptwriting, voice-overs, and background music, I have, as of this writing, completed four videos. One video was of a kitchen remodel my husband helped our contractor friend do, and another was a recap of our family summer. One was of the breeze moving leaves across a pond. Just silly stuff, really. I haven't received a ton of feedback from my friends, but even without it, I know there has been marked improvement. The camera shake has been virtually eliminated, and I've learned enough of the video-editing software that the colors on the final versions of my videos aren't as dull as they once were.

Sure, there's still a long way to go, and Martin Scorsese won't feel threatened by my filmmaking skills anytime soon. But I'm not embarrassed by my work, either. And man oh man, I am *loving* the process. The more I learn, the more I *want* to learn. I love figuring out how to shoot interesting angles, and I lose track of time when I am fiddling around with my video-editing software. Contrary to my initial cockiness, it's clear that I'm still at the starting line, but I'm up for the challenge.

And I have big, big plans, too. I want to upgrade my gear—maybe a new camera and a gimbal, and definitely some more advanced video-processing software. I also want to see if I can incorporate my still photography into my little films. And maybe animation! It'd be really cool to see if I could add animation *on top of* my stills, and splice them seamlessly with the motion footage. . . .

You get my point. The idea of seeing where these little films can go excites me—even if I never receive any feedback from friends, even if no one ever sees these films but me. Filmmaking is providing me all the improvisational and experimentation potential I could ever want, and I really don't want the fun to end.

Huh. Maybe I've remembered how to play after all.

stretch zone

Stretch Zone

The Only Way to Do It Is to Do It

YEARS AGO, I was sitting in my home office in front of my computer, processing a few photographs. Marcus and Alex were around, and each of us was in a different part of the house, doing our own thing.

Suddenly, a breaking news alert from CNN's Twitter account popped up in the corner of my screen:

@CNNBRK: Diana Nyad about 2 miles from end of Cuba-to-Florida swim, team says.

Wait, what? *Swim?* I clicked on the included link.

Sure enough, there was a live helicopter feed of a woman in a blue swim cap and swimsuit, laboriously doing the crawl in the turquoise waters off the coast of the Florida Keys. A boat nearby appeared to be monitoring her every stroke. But otherwise, she was a solitary figure in the vast expanse of ocean.

As I watched, I learned that Diana Nyad was an endurance swimmer who had failed to complete this distance four times earlier. This fifth time, however, it appeared she was going to make it. If she did, she'd be the first person ever to swim across the Florida Straits from Cuba to Florida without a shark cage. *At sixty-four years old.*

"Marcus, Alex, come see this, quick!"

They both came running. "This woman has just swum over one hundred miles from Cuba," I gushed. "She's the first person *ever* to do this. There were sharks and jellyfish, and she just kept swimming, with no assistance, no stopping, for more than two days. And she's about to make it to Florida!"

"Oh. Cool." They stood politely looking over my shoulder at the screen for a brief moment, before quietly returning to whatever it was they were doing.

I guess they weren't that impressed.

But I was transfixed. For the next ninety minutes, I stared at my laptop as the newscasters provided commentary about this extraordinary feat. As she neared the shore, folks on paddleboards and in small sailboats appeared (it was Labor Day, after all, a quintessential beach day, if ever there is one). They formed a path guiding her toward land, all while cheering her name.

By the time she could stand up in the water, a huge crowd had arrived, including news crews and other journalists. For the swim to be officially recorded as unassisted, however, no one could touch her until she was on dry land. Members of her team formed a wide circle around her, yelling "Don't touch her!" while keeping the crowds a safe distance away. She staggered weakly, her face and lips swollen and encrusted with salt.

Finally, her feet hit dry land. She collapsed into the arms of her best friend, Bonnie Stoll, who had served as the head handler for this expedition. The crowd, now numbering in the thousands, erupted into loud cheers.

And I burst into tears. *She's amazing*, I thought, watching the medics rush to her side with a stretcher.

And then, my second thought: *Why in God's name would anyone go out of their comfort zone like that?*

With few exceptions, I've spent most of my life doing decidedly undaring things. Preferably somewhere cozy. Ideally, with a cup of tea. What I'm saying is my friend Maggie from Chapter 2 might prefer parasailing to paragliding, but I promise you that when she shared her story with me, neither sounded particularly appealing.

So, as someone who is deeply attached to her comfort zone, I low-key resent anyone who tells me that I should move from it. I mean, *why?* Who decided this was a good thing to do? Comfort zones are cozy, like warm, snuggly blankets. You all have a good time outside of your comfort zone, I'll stay right here, thankyouverymuch.

Still, there's a part of me that has long wondered if, in my reluctance to venture too far outside of my comfort zone, I might be doing myself a disservice. Julia Cameron, the author of *The Artist's Way*, puts it this way: "A little risk-taking is enlivening, because it helps expand our self-definition."

This self-definition derives from the culmination of *all* the experiences in our lives, so I suspected that closing myself off to expansive experiences was likely doing nothing for my self-definition's growth. Even more, research suggests that when we step outside of our comfort zones, we become more resilient. Our awareness of the world expands, as does our understanding of how we fit in it. And finally, we give ourselves *agency*; we learn more about ourselves and understand the power we each have to create the lives we want.

Okay, I get it: Pushing ourselves to do something that feels a bit scary is a *good* thing. But still: What Diana Nyad did seems like the very definition of true madness.

Except . . . what if she never actually left her comfort zone in the first place?

Kristen Butler, author of the book *The Comfort Zone: Create a Life You Really Love with Less Stress and More Flow*, offers a new perspective on this notion of our comfort zone. She distinguishes it from our "complacency zone": the mindset in which our self-talk sounds like, "I'm fine where I am. Why try for anything more? It's pointless to dream, because hope leads to disappointment." We're hanging out in the complacency zone when we watch an expert skillfully practice an activity and think, "I'd look like an idiot if I did that." We're in our complacency zone when we dismiss an idea of attempting something new out of hand—even as a small part of us wonders what might happen if only we'd try.

Our comfort zone, on the other hand, is where we feel secure enough to dare expand. "When you operate from your Comfort Zone," writes Butler, "you listen to your own inner guidance rather than to the suggestions of others. You create healthy boundaries and they are honored. As a result, you start living life your way, rather than following someone else's road map for you."

I love this reframing. Maybe our comfort zone isn't about *stagnation*, as it's often described, or something we need to *get out of*. Maybe it's a zone of safety that allows us to get curious about what we might be able to accomplish if we set our minds to it. To wonder what we're made of, and then take steps to find out.

This, of course, is exactly what Diana Nyad did. She didn't suddenly don a swimsuit, snap on a swim cap, and dive into the waters off the coast of Havana. She had years—*decades,* even—of endurance swimming experience, including being known in the 1970s as the world's greatest long-distance swimmer. (This was, in part, thanks to a record-breaking swim around the island of Manhattan.)

And although she was alone in the water, she wasn't alone in the ocean: There was an entire team with her every stroke of the way, giving her fresh water to drink, as well as nourishment and encouragement. She had built-in safety and experience that freed her to expand her comfort zone. As a result, once completed, her self-definition had evolved:

"I've sat down with Oprah, and I've been in President Obama's Oval Office," she said. "I'm proud of it all, but the truth is, I'm walking around tall because I am [a] bold, fearless person, and I will be, every day, until it's time for these days to be done."

Talk about becoming more interesting!

The idea of never having to actually *leave* your comfort zone in order to expand it intrigued me. What if intentional amateurism involves not getting out of your comfort zone but simply stretching it, bit by bit, until it's roomy enough to contain something new and risky and brave?

I thought about this when a few years later and a little closer to home, I was talking with my friend Aimee Woodall. During our conversation, she shared her own story with me about expanding her comfort zone . . . all by taking a long walk in the woods.

The Appalachian Trail is a meandering route along the Eastern Seaboard of the United States, from Georgia to Maine. It is apparently the world's longest hiking-only trail. And I couldn't believe I'd known Aimee a decade before I learned she had once walked the entirety of its 2,200 miles. Alone.

It's not that I didn't think she was capable of such a feat. It just never dawned on me that it was something Aimee, the CEO of a successful brand strategy and creative agency in Houston, would ever be interested in doing. She admits that when she embarked on her walk, taking months off to trek in the wilderness seemed out of character to her, as well.

Aimee told me she'd found out about the trail years earlier, sitting on a bar stool having lunch in North Carolina. Two backpackers had come in and sat down next to her. "I had never even heard of the Appalachian Trail, but by the end of our conversation, I was just completely enamored," she told me. "It sounded like an adventure that I could be capable of, given that I had two working legs and an active body. Besides, I love the mountains. So years later, when I was looking for something to do to reset myself after an important relationship crumbled, I remembered that conversation."

Here's the amazing thing: At the time she decided to hike the Appalachian Trail, Aimee had never really hiked before. If you're planning to through-hike the entirety of the trail from the southernmost point to the northern end, as Aimee planned to do, you have to start by a certain time of year so that you can get off the trail before winter sets in. The last thing a trail hiker does is summit Mount Katahdin in Maine, and with snowfall, it isn't safe to climb the mountain. By the time Aimee had made the decision to go, there were only about four weeks left before she had to get started. If she was going to finish before winter, she had to plan quickly.

So she bought a pair of hiking boots and then broke them in by walking around the house.

"Okay, so let me get this straight," I said. "Just weeks after making the decision to go, you fly to Georgia to begin this trek with your new gear and barely broken-in hiking boots. And you're all alone? Talk about being out of your comfort zone! Weren't you scared?"

"I was scared, but because everyone was telling me I was crazy to do it, I was mostly just energized by their doubting me," Aimee said. "Besides, there was really no time to second-guess what I was doing. There was a timeline, and if I was going to make it to Mount Katahdin in time, I needed to just get going."

"It sounds like your attitude was 'I'm going to summit that damn mountain at the end of the trail and show everyone I can do it.'"

Aimee thought for a second. "If I'm being honest, what was going through my head at the time was 'I'm going to summit that damn mountain at the end of the trail and show *myself* I could do it."

"Oh. That's an important distinction," I said.

"Right. Also, what's the worst that could happen? I could get off the trail and go home at any time. But I was in the middle of a big transition and going back home wasn't enticing, so the reward of staying was much more powerful than the idea of giving up."

This is critical: Aimee's belief that she could stop at any time created a safety net for her, a mindset that freed her to take the risk. By believing in her ability to call things off whenever she needed to, she gave herself the space to stretch herself and expand her comfort zone.

"You mentioned that the entire experience was life-changing," I said. "What did the trail teach you?"

Aimee didn't even hesitate in her answer: "My greatest learning is that it's possible to just go for it." As she recalled her experience on the trail, her eyes twinkled, and she added, "I know that if you believe something is possible, and you're willing to wake up every day and believe in it again, then it can be done."

"But there's another thing," she continued. "The other lesson the trail taught me, one that I think about probably fifteen times a day, is that anything can be achieved by putting one foot in front of the other. I mean, I've *lived* this metaphor: I walked fourteen states and 2,200 miles, and I did it because I literally put one foot in front of the other. Because of this, I really honed my ability to break down huge, overwhelming, and intimidating projects into smaller, manageable tasks."

I asked Aimee if she would do it all again if she had the chance.

"I don't know," she said, ruminating a bit. "I don't feel I *have* to. It served me for that particular moment in time. But the Appalachian Trail definitely turned me into a *hiker*. Isn't that crazy? I did this huge thing on a whim, and it turned out that I *love* it. So, while I might not do a multi-month trail hike again anytime soon, I do find myself wanting to integrate hiking into my life as much as possible."

What a lovely expansion of her self-identity. By playing with the edges of her comfort zone, Aimee discovered an avocation that she happily practices to this day with her partner and their young children. She's now a total amateur hiker, in the best possible way.

After speaking with Aimee about her epic hike, I couldn't stop thinking about our conversation. I had no desire to do anything similar. The way I see it, if God wanted us to spend any part of our precious lives hiking and camping, She wouldn't have invented "indoors."

But Aimee's story inspired me to explore the edges of my comfort zone. Maybe I could try something that always seemed fun, but I'd never been brave enough to attempt. Something that, once pursued, might help me feel more courageous. More interesting. More badass.

Which is why one day, a few months later, I heard these words coming out of my mouth: "While we're here, I want to take surfing lessons."

Marcus looked at me like I'd just grown a second head. When we met more than twenty years earlier, he had been an avid body surfer, surfing up and down the Cornish coast of England. Back then, as he donned his wetsuit and helmet (lest he crash into the boulders that lined the beach), he never understood why I'd preferred to remain on dry land, shivering in my heavy wool coat, hat, and gloves, patiently waiting for him to finish. But I, with my Caribbean blood, wouldn't even think about setting foot in the cold waters of the Northern Atlantic, much less surf in it.

But this time, we weren't in the Northern Atlantic; we were on a family vacation in Cabo San Lucas, Mexico, and the temperature was hovering at a sunny 82 degrees Fahrenheit. Attempting to surf had been on my life list for years, and it had now migrated its way to my Amateur's Menu. I thought of Aimee's adventure, and how the mountains called to her; the truth is, the ocean had always called to *me*. Besides, we learned through research before our trip that Cabo San Lucas is a top destination for beginner surfers, due to its combination of gentle waves, stunning scenery, and friendly surf culture. If that didn't sound like the perfect setting to try to expand my comfort zone, I don't know what did.

After Marcus got over his shock, we asked Marta, our hotel's concierge, if she could find us a surf school for beginners. This was a challenging request: It was a holiday weekend in the United States, and many Americans had headed south for their days off. This meant that many surf schools were booked. But Marta was persistent, and after hours of searching, she found an establishment that had enough safety certifications to satisfy her. "This is your first time, yes?" she asked, looking directly at me. "Then we're going to be safe."

Two days later, we were sitting in our rental car parked on the beach, about to meet our surf instructor Francisco, and his son, Josue. Marcus looked over at me. "Are you ready?" he smiled.

"What if I die?" I responded.

"You're not going to die," he sighed.

"You don't know that."

"You're being silly. Get out of the car."

I persisted. "I just want you to know that if I die, I loved being married to you."

"Get out of the car."

Reluctantly, I got out.

The ocean, it must be said, was perfect: vibrant blue, with waves rolling and breaking in a slow cadence, one after the other. It was early morning, but already there were about a dozen surfers out on the water, taking long, lazy runs on the moderately sized waves that rolled to the shore. I stared at them, impressed, until Francisco broke the spell.

"Here, put this on," he said, handing me a rash vest, "and come this way." Marcus and I put on our vests and followed Francisco to where two epoxy longboards were lying on the sand.

Francisco dropped to his knees and began drawing.

"This line represents the beach," he said, running his finger in the sand, "and this represents the sea. See this?" He drew a parallel line and pointed to it. "*This* is a line of rocks in the shallows. You're going to want to ditch your board before you get to this point. Because if your board pulls you here when you get off. . . . " Here he dragged his fingernails across his face.

Jesus.

"Okay, now the boards." He motioned to Josue, who laid face down on one of the boards to demonstrate. "See how his toes are at the end of the board? That's where you should be."

Francisco and Josue demonstrated the proper technique for about ten minutes, making us copy them so they could evaluate our form. Then Francisco strapped the boards to our left ankles.

"Okay, let's get in the water," he said. "Time to surf."

"Say what, now?!" I said, alarmed.

"Only way you're going to do it is to do it," Francisco grinned. "I'll be right beside you."

We waded into the water and hopped onto the boards. "Start paddling out to those surfers over there."

I began paddling and was surprised to find the board actually moving in the right direction. *That's one concern conquered*, I thought. I had been convinced I wouldn't be strong enough to paddle out and that the waves would just wash me and my board to shore. Soon enough, though, I was floating alongside the other surfers.

Also, I was completely out of breath.

"Okay, Marcus, you go first," shouted Francisco. Josue had swum out without his surfboard, and was right next to me, hanging on to mine. Now he was orienting my board toward the shore. I watched as Marcus maneuvered his board into place.

Suddenly Francisco shouted: "PADDLE! PADDLE! PADDLE!"

Marcus obeyed, paddling furiously as a wave took him and his board. He tried to pop up but rolled over to his side, and the wave crashed over him. He surfaced, grinning.

"Your turn," murmured Josue, with a kind smile.

I took a deep breath, my heart suddenly pounding in my chest.

About ten seconds passed. And then: "PADDLE! PADDLE! PADDLE!"

I did as I was told, paddling as hard as I could and unsure of when I was supposed to do the next step. At first, the board didn't seem to move . . .

. . . until suddenly it did.

If you've never been on a surfboard before, I'm not sure if I can fully describe the feeling when the wave grabs it. It's as if some unknown force guns an invisible engine, and the board suddenly surges forward faster than you thought possible. I popped up into plank position, but then became alarmed at how quickly the shore was rushing toward me. I thought of Francisco's drawing of the rocks near shore, and his pantomime of being scratched across the face. With considerable panic, I rolled off the board and into the water.

Just because I'd stopped surfing, however, didn't mean my board did. As the wave crashed over me, I felt the headwrap I'd used to tie my hair back fly off my head. By some miracle, I caught it. But as I was congratulating myself for my deftness, the cord tethering the board to my ankle suddenly yanked. *Hard.*

Ah shit, I thought, as my body jerked halfway out of the water like a rag doll, and I felt my back cry out in protest.

And then it was over.

I stood up, completely breathless, my heart still pounding. Francisco appeared out of nowhere. "Are you okay? Where's your scarf?"

Unable to speak, I raised my right hand to show him my scarf.

"You caught it! Amazing! Let's go again! Come on! Paddle out!"

This, by the way, was genius on Francisco's part: Before I could figure out whether I was scared or overwhelmed, Francisco was positioning my board for me to begin paddling out to sea. I hopped back on the board and began paddling, joined by a still-smiling Josue. He grabbed my board and began turning it to shore.

"Are you ready to go again?"

At this point I was completely out of breath, spent from the journey back to the sea. "Puedo descansar un momentito?" *Can I rest for a minute?*

"Sí! Sí! Descanse!"

I double-wrapped my scarf around my wrist and lay my head down on the board, slowing my breathing down as much as possible. I was scared, but also exhilarated. *I tried it*, I thought to myself. *I tried it and I didn't die. I think I can try it again.*

After about forty-five seconds, I looked at Josue and nodded.

"Ready?" he asked, positioning the board.

"Ready," I said. "Let's go."

I lay on the board facing the shore, as Josue looked behind us out to sea. I watched as he shook his head almost imperceptibly and a swell rolled under us. We rose and fell with the water.

"Next one," he murmured, not taking his eyes off the ocean.

Fifteen more seconds passed.

"Okay, PADDLE! PADDLE! PADDLE!"

Again, I obeyed, paddling furiously, except this time I knew what to expect. I felt the wave come roaring behind me and felt the sudden jolt of acceleration.

I popped up into plank position and took a giant step forward. There was I was in a low squat, hurtling toward shore.

I'm doing it! I thought. *All I have to do is stand up!*

I froze.

Stand! I silently shouted to myself. Nothing happened. As I stayed in a squat, I remembered the rocky shore and Francisco pantomiming jagged scratches on his face.

It's too late! I threw myself off the board, and the wave crashed over me. Again, the board yanked my leg hard, jerking my body violently forward. I popped to the surface, and again, Francisco was right by my side.

"You okay?" he asked, grinning his high-wattage grin.

"Yes," I said, "but . . . "

"Let's go again!" Just as he spoke, another wave came crashing to the shore. The board pulled my leg again, and I lost my balance. "I think I need a break!" I shouted.

"Give me your foot!" Francisco yelled back. I raised my ankle toward him, and with one swift motion, he untethered the board. He brought it close to me as I regained my footing. The rocks were sharp under my feet.

"Can you make it to the beach?"

"I think so," I said, grabbing the board. "Yes."

I dragged my board to the sand where we'd left our stuff and sank into a folding chair. I was completely out of breath, but I was exhilarated. I looked out at the ocean just in time to see Marcus stand all the way up on his board—and stay there, for about a second and a half!—before finally ditching into the waves. I whooped loudly, and he waved with a laugh.

About five minutes later, he joined me on the beach. "You did it!" I exclaimed. "You were up!"

"I was up!" he grinned. "And then I panicked because I didn't know what to do next!"

I laughed. "Me too!" I said. "I got into a squat and then froze."

"Well, we both got to our feet," he said, raising his hand for a high five. "Yay, us!"

"How many times did you go?" I asked.

"That last time was my third."

"Are you going again?"

"Hell no," he said. "I'm so exhausted. That took so much out of me."

I almost cried with relief. "Oh, thank God," I said. "I'm completely wiped out after going twice. I thought you'd think I was pathetic."

"No, it's exhausting for sure, if you're not used to it. Just paddling out is a workout."

"It was incredible, though," I said. "I definitely want to do this again. Maybe we can find a surf camp sometime."

Marcus looked at me. "Really? You loved it?"

I nodded. "I loved it. Like, I might love it more than I love scuba diving, and you *know* I love scuba diving."

Marcus and I sat there on the beach for the rest of the morning, watching the surfers catch wave after wave. I was exhilarated. And I was proud of myself for trying. I had actually gotten to my feet! Before I knew it, I was already plotting my next surf trip. I had no illusions of becoming an expert surfer; my back was really sore and would remain achy for three weeks afterward. But just like that, my comfort zone had stretched and my self-definition had expanded. In four hours, I had gone from being a person who had never surfed before to a person who loved surfing.

And that feeling of the ocean grabbing me and sailing along its surface? Well, I knew that one day, I had to capture that feeling again.

connection

Connection

Getting Your Essential Vitamin

BINDHU VINODHAN HAD recently transformed her life in a seismic way. Formerly a high-powered executive who'd led human resources, organizational effectiveness, and DEI teams at some of the largest companies in the world, Bindhu left her corporate life to create the Mauna Dhwani Foundation, supporting the women of the tribal villages of Odisha, India. Bindhu's goal and the goal of her foundation is to ensure each woman earns a sustainable living wage while working within a caring, empowering community. The artisans of her enterprise create gorgeous crafts, using local dyes and weaving storytelling motifs into their work.

I met Bindhu when I was in New York City, mentoring in a leadership program designed to help women entrepreneurs grow their businesses. The women in this program were focused on creating a global market for the indigenous communities of their homelands by preserving and amplifying the traditional craftsmanship of their people.

To say it was an honor to be in their midst would be an understatement.

The program began with each woman introducing herself, and on the second day of the summit, they took over a conference room, each displaying her organization's products. I stopped in front of Bindu's table, where she was wearing a sari that featured the traditional weaving techniques of the Odisha community. As I looked through her collection, I noticed a striking blue scarf hanging on a rack. Dyed with indigo, the scarf had edges hand embroidered with red thread and pink beads. A white motif of twin fish was woven throughout the fabric. Bindhu explained that the message of the scarf was encoded in its pattern: The twin fish meant "you never walk alone." I bought it on the spot.

A few hours later, Bindhu approached me. "I spoke with Meeta," she said in her soft-spoken way. "Meeta is the person who wove your scarf. You're the first person who has purchased anything she has ever made."

"Whoa! That's amazing!" I said.

"She was asking about you: what you looked like, and where you lived. And I was wondering . . ." Here, Bindu became shy. "Well, would you be open to meeting with her via video call tomorrow morning?"

I was elated. "Are you kidding? It would be my absolute honor."

The next day, I arrived at the program venue extra early, ready to meet Meeta. Naturally, I wore her scarf. Bindhu called the manager of her weavers' cooperative in Odisha, India, and suddenly a face appeared on her phone screen.

She's so young, I thought. "Hello, Meeta!" I said. "My name is Karen. It's so nice to meet you!"

"Thank you," she said in English, putting her hands in prayer position and raising them to her forehead, bowing slightly.

"I love my scarf," I said, touching the beading with my fingers. "It's so beautiful. You're very talented."

Bindhu translated. "Thank you," Meeta said again.

"How old are you?" Bindhu relayed my question. This time, Meeta responded in her native language. Bindhu said, "She's nineteen."

For a moment, Meeta sat in uncomfortable silence. I continued smiling at her, wondering what I should ask her next. Then Meeta spoke. Bindhu listened, and then turned to me. "She's asking if she can show you her loom."

"Absolutely!" I said, smiling and nodding at the young face on the screen. "I'd love to see your loom."

Meeta rose from her chair and went inside a bright orange building that had walls decorated with indigenous patterns in white paint. She approached a large loom, where a scarf similar to the one I was wearing was in progress. She sat at the loom, and then turned to face the camera.

It was at this moment that Meeta's demeanor changed. The timid girl who first greeted me was now replaced by a confident young woman. I learned later that Bindhu's organization had rescued Meeta from sex trafficking. It was clear that the loom was more than just a tool of her craft. For Meeta, it represented freedom. Independence. Pride.

"What city do you live in?" asked Meeta, through Bindhu.

"I live in a city called Houston, in the United States," I answered.

She asked about my family, and I told her I'm married to a man named Marcus and that we have a daughter named Alex. "She's not much older than you," I said.

"How old is she?"

"She's twenty." I smiled. "She's at university, but she can't make beautiful scarves like you do."

Meeta squared her shoulders and responded with dancing eyes. Bindhu laughed softly.

"What did she say?" I asked.

"She said that maybe one day you and your daughter will come to India, and she will teach Alex how to weave."

I grinned. "Meeta, that would be so wonderful," I said. "And it would give me so much pleasure to meet you in person."

A few minutes later, the cell phone connection began to fail, and we had to say our goodbyes. After we hung up, both Bindhu and I were overwhelmed with emotion.

"Bindhu! She was so confident sitting at her loom! Look at the amazing work you're doing!"

Bindhu's eyes sparkled. "You're the first person she's ever spoken to outside of her village," she said.

"Well, she's the first person I've ever spoken to in India," I said, wiping away my own tears.

Our conversation, with Meeta speaking with her very first customer, may have been a pivotal moment in her life, but it was a pivotal moment in my life as well. There's something so meaningful when, despite distance and language barriers and dodgy cellular service, two people can find connection. I don't know if or when I will be able to travel with my daughter all the way to Odisha, but Lord knows that after my time with Meeta, I'm sure going to try. After our conversation, I feel like a part of her is with me, especially every time I wear her gorgeous scarf. The twin fish in the scarf's motif remind me that when we make a connection with someone, we leave something of ourselves with them, as they do with us.

Truly, we never walk alone.

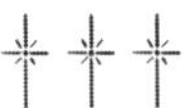

My time with Meeta was short, only about fifteen minutes. But there was no denying that those moments resulted in a feeling of profound kinship. Of course, this isn't surprising. Dr. Edward Hallowell, a board-certified psychiatrist, and author of the book *Connect: 12 Vital Ties that Open Your Heart, Lengthen Your Life, and Deepen Your Soul*, would describe my conversation with Meeta as a "human moment."

"A human moment," he writes, "occurs any time two or more people are together, paying attention to one another." Human moments are what lead to *connection*, which he further defines as "feeling a part of something larger than yourself, and feeling welcome and understood." This is exactly what happened between Meeta and me: Despite the distance and language barrier, we were curious about each other, and—with Bindhu's intercession—we felt understood and part of the bigger world.

Human moments don't have to be fleeting. My friend Camille van Hoegaerden experienced connection in an even more profound and concentrated way. Camille asked an acquaintance—someone with whom she was friendly but barely knew—to accompany her on a walk along the South West Coast Path in the United Kingdom. But it wasn't an afternoon hike or even a weekend trip. The path is 630 miles, and walking it takes ten weeks.

Camille had met Lindsey when they joined a group of volunteers to transform some open land next to Camille's yoga studio into a field of flowers. "Although I originally thought I'd undertake the walk as a solo pilgrimage of sorts, there was also a part of me that felt learning to journey in the company of others was just as, if not more, important," Camille told me. "Lindsey is older than I am, so we're in different phases of life, but her energy is calm and supportive, and so I asked her to come along. I thought having her with me would make the walk seem . . . I don't know, *lighter*."

They made the decision to go on the walk quickly, with no time to train. Two weeks after Camille extended her invitation to Lindsey, the two set off from Minehead, on the northern coast of the English county of Somerset. "We were bubbly and excited," Camille remembers. "We really didn't know what we were doing, but for some reason, we weren't nervous. We just figured that we'd learn along the way, because if we overthought it, it would stress us both out."

The walk provided two months' worth of Dr. Hallowell's "human moments." "We did so much laughing. *So much laughing*," Camille recounts. "I remember in the evenings we would sit side-by-side outside our tents, warm mugs of tea in hand, and recount our day as night crept in—particularly the small moments of kindness from strangers, or the hilarity of the elements that didn't quite go to plan. There was a loveliness in the support we provided for each other as well: If I had a blister, Lindsey would whip out a plaster from her pack, and if she was having a moment of self-doubt, I would remind her of all the qualities I so admired in her. I'll never forget the night my tent broke during a storm, and Lindsey welcomed me into her shelter. We lay head to toe like sardines, the wind whipping around us until morning, when the storm passed. There was a bond of protection and safety between us."

During the walk, Camille and Lindsey didn't use social media, which allowed them to be entirely focused on the experience they were having with each other. "Looking back in hindsight, I realize that really, although we walked the same path and shared each other's company, we were each on our own journey," Camille said. "And of course, now Lindsey is a dear, dear friend, and we'll likely do more walks together in the future."

In this amateur hiking adventure with her new friend, Camille had stumbled on how nurturing connection is good for our well-being. This is true even if we're not doing it along the beautiful English coast. This aspect of our welfare, what we could think of as "social health," is not talked about nearly as much as mental and physical health are. Coined by social scientist Kalsey Killam, the term *social health* means "the aspect of overall health and well-being that comes from connection—and it is vastly underappreciated." So underappreciated, apparently, that the lack of social health in the United States alone has risen to alarming levels.

Dr. Vivek Murthy, surgeon general of the United States under both the Obama and Biden administrations, has made the study of loneliness—the antithesis of social health—one of the hallmarks of his work. In his book *Together: The Healing Power of Human Connection in an Often Lonely World*, he describes embarking on a listening tour of the United States when he was first named surgeon general, and his surprising findings. "Loneliness ran like a dark thread through many of the more obvious issues that people brought to my attention," he writes, "like addiction, violence, anxiety and depression."

The situation has become so critical that during Dr. Murthy's tenure in 2023, the Office of the Surgeon General issued a health advisory, entitled "Our Epidemic of Loneliness and Isolation." This lack of social connection dangerously affects our quality of life; in fact, Dr. Murthy spelled out exactly what's at risk when we don't nourish our social health. "People with strong social relationships are fifty percent less likely to die prematurely than people with weak social relationships," he writes. "Even more striking . . . the impact of lacking social connection on reducing lifespan is equal to the risk of smoking fifteen cigarettes a day, and it's *greater* than the risk associated with obesity, excess alcohol consumption and lack of exercise."

But there's good news: Social connection is in our nature. Dr. Murthy writes, "the human need for social connection is more than a simple feeling or convenience—it's a biological and social imperative rooted in thousands of years of human evolution." He continues: "Our ancestors' default setting was togetherness." Dr. Hallowell agrees: "Connection is an essential vitamin," he writes. "You can't live without it."

Connection is so fundamental to healthy living that it makes sense to be intentional about nurturing our relationships as much as possible. Just as we move our bodies to take care of our physical health, so too should we cultivate and nurture our connections to take care of our social health. Luckily, because we're wired for social connection, there are simple ways to make sure we make social health a priority. Based on her research, Killam recommends a few strategies: Try to connect with five different people every week, she says. Maintain at least three close relationships in general. And finally, dedicate at least one hour each day to social interaction.

To be clear, these relationships can be diverse: They can be friends, parents, children, partners, whoever. The even better news? The way in which we nurture these relationships can include practicing our intentional amateurism, as Camille did on her walk with Lindsey. "One of the best ways to strengthen your social muscles is to do what you love with others," writes Killam. "Research shows that time and intimacy have a linear correlation: the more time you spend with someone, the closer you become."

In other words, there's no reason we have to enjoy the things we love alone. The more we create opportunities for human moments to arise, as we practice intentional amateurism doing the things we love, the more our connections grow and the healthier we become.

An admission: As a profound introvert (a fact confirmed by plumb near every personality test that exists), I feel some trepidation about this attribute of intentional amateurism. I love when human moments arise organically, as happened with Meeta. But unless I'm invited (as I was with Meeta), the idea of intentionally nurturing connections sounds, well, like a lot of *work* to introverts like me. Taking the initiative to create connection doesn't come particularly naturally to some of us. So I decided that if I was going to do this human-moment-connection thing, I would begin by focusing on one of my most important relationships: the one with my partner, Marcus.

Alex had recently left for university, and on a quick weekend trip to a cabin in the woods to celebrate our new-found "open nest," Marcus had shared his dream with me of one day learning to sail. This was news: I knew that soon after graduating high school, Marcus had worked as a chef on a dive boat off the coast of England, but I didn't know that sailing had been on his life list since then. So after our weekend away, I began searching for sailing schools in our area. I found a reputable one and registered us both for the introductory sailing course.

The night before the course, I was so excited that I foolishly searched YouTube for a rudimentary "how-to-sail" video. The one I landed on was about twenty-five minutes long, the perfect amount of time to become alarmed by the sheer number of wholly unfamiliar terms: "Let's get in our close haul position: I'm gonna pull the main sheet—too much, fall off the wind, let it catch, there we go—now, we want to go right past the point where the sail is luffing . . ." Seriously, was this man speaking in tongues?

By the time the video was over, I was convinced that there was no way I was going to remember anything I was taught. I also had a new fear that I'd be pitched into the water by what I had just learned was called a "swinging boom."

My anxiety was not alleviated when, on the following day, I found myself on a boat dock in Seabrook, Texas, reading the following sign:

NOTICE

> *Alligators are common in this area. They can be dangerous and should not be approached, frightened or fed. Please give them the respect they deserve KEEP YOUR DISTANCE*

Wild-eyed, I glanced at Marcus. He rolled his eyes. "Woman, get on the boat," he said over his shoulder. I glared at his back as he eagerly made his way down the gangway behind the rest of the students who'd registered for the same class. *If he remains this unsympathetic, I'll give* him *a "human moment,"* I thought, and followed behind.

We climbed aboard, six of us would-be mariners in all, and situated ourselves on the seats along the edge of the sailboat. I sat next to a woman who was carrying a small backpack with "Methodist Hospital" emblazoned on its side. "Are you a doctor?" I asked.

"Nurse," she corrected, smiling.

"Great. So, in your medical opinion, will *this*"—I held up one of the shabby life vests they'd given each of us at the sailing school office—"actually save our lives?"

"Absolutely not," she answered, not missing a beat. "Also, I can't swim. So if it all goes south, I'll be counting on you to save me."

"Oh, you're not going to need those." A man with a leathery face and a low, growly voice interrupted with an amused smile. "I'm not sure why they gave them to you. There are vests under your seats if you need them. Those are just for when you're getting certified on the smaller boats."

The gravel-voiced man introduced himself as our captain. "It's a good day for a sail," he said. "We're going to go out into the bay for a few hours. You can stow your bags in the cabin to give yourself more room on deck. The bathroom—what we call the "head"—is also in the cabin. But it's a bit tricky: The only thing that should go in there is what comes out of your body. Toilet paper goes in the trash can."

Jesus.

The captain was a man of few words. Silently, he untied the boat, hopped on board, started the inboard motor, and we made our way out of the docks. We passed lots of other boats doing the same thing—it seemed no one wanted to waste the beautiful fall weather—before we finally made it out of the channel and into the bay.

After about fifteen minutes, the captain cut the motor. Working quickly, he loosened a line, and the jib unfurled at the bow of the boat (*look at me, using sailing words!*). The wind caught the sail, and suddenly, all was quiet.

"We're sailing," said the captain. "Anyone want to take the helm?"

The winds and seas were calm, so we were all game to have a go. When it was my turn, I nervously took the wheel. "Which way?"

"Straight ahead," said the captain, which suited me just fine. Occasionally, I'd give the wheel a slight turn, just to feel how the boat responded, and then turn it back. The captain didn't freak out, so I relaxed. When Marcus took his turn, he was beaming. It was as if, being on the ocean, he'd rediscovered the place his soul was meant to be.

The sun rose higher in the sky, and the group of us became comfortable, introducing ourselves to each other and chatting easily. Together we watched pelicans as they dive-bombed the ocean for a fishy snack, and pods of dolphins breaking the water's surface as they followed the boat.

Four hours flew by, and all too soon it was time to make our way back to the docks in Seabrook. Once the boat was tied off, we thanked the captain profusely for a perfect day ("Don't mention it," he gruffed, before turning to clean the boat). Marcus and I said goodbye to our motley crew of fellow students. I assured the nurse that had she fallen overboard, I would have jumped in to save her. (Not really. I'm not that strong of a swimmer—I'm a turtle, remember? But I would've sent Marcus after her.)

As Marcus and I walked past the alligator sign to where our car was parked, I told him we should officially sign up to get our basic keelboat licenses.

He grinned. "Definitely. That was amazing."

"I agree," I said, nodding. "But you have to promise me that once we're licensed, if we ever charter a boat to sail, it will have a head with toilet paper that can *flush*."

"Done." Marcus shuddered. "Even *I* can't deal with a trash can full of used toilet paper. That's just nasty."

As soon as we were back at the school headquarters, we signed up for the Basic Keelboat Certification course, where we'd learn to skipper a twenty-six-foot boat. As Marcus paid, I eagerly thumbed through the brand-new textbooks they'd handed us for our course. Somehow, now that we'd actually sailed, the sailing terms seemed less intimidating and more intriguing. On the entire forty-minute drive back into Houston, we couldn't stop talking about our experience on the boat and dreaming about taking Alex or other members of our family out on the water with us.

And it was at this point, I understood: When we do amateur things with other amateurs, the opportunities for the human moments that Dr. Hallowell writes about abound, and not just in the practice alone. The sailing course itself, as fun as it was, wasn't the only human moment. The human moments continued long after, on the drive back and even later, as we continued to reminisce about the day. It is the face-to-face interactions, both in the doing and the recollecting, and the way that they contribute to a sense of psychological security and happiness that make connection so powerful. And what better way to inspire these face-to-face interactions, these human moments, than by practicing amateurism, by being willing to fail, by being vulnerable, *together*? As vulnerability and shame researcher Dr. Brené Brown writes, this type of vulnerability is open and mutual, and an integral part of the trust-building process—therefore, it increases connection.

As of this writing, Marcus and I have yet to take our sailing licensing course, but we're determined to make it happen. We continue to dream about what adventures may lie ahead. Will we one day charter a boat and sail all along the Texas shore? Will we take sailing vacations to far-away lands? *Will we ever find head-friendly toilet paper?*

Time will tell. But for me, the biggest lesson, by far, was how easy it is—even for my introverted soul—to create fertile ground for human moments to happen. All I had to do was pay attention to the people I love and think of activities we might love to do together. And by choosing interests I love, the idea of engaging others to be amateurs along with me somehow feels far less intimidating, and far more exciting. Imagine the lightness we could create together as we dabbled in new hobbies and pastimes!

And the beauty is that even when we're not good at them, the connections we make together are a great reminder that we needn't ever walk alone.

awe

Wonder and Awe

Trenches, Hummingbirds, and Fuzzy Stars

ONCE UPON A time, years ago, I took myself on a solo vacation. I'd been living in London for several months and the constant cold, gray days had finally gotten to me. My Caribbean soul craved sun and sand, and a vacation to Grand Cayman seemed like just the ticket to sweep my rain-induced blues away. "I'll take a stack of books and read on the beach," I thought to myself. "And if I really need to socialize, I'll sign up for a dive trip."

My brand-spanking-new scuba diving certification card had afforded me the opportunity to go on a handful of very easy dives before I'd moved to London, and I was eager to do more. For this Cayman adventure, I'd researched the best dive operation on the island, and on my first morning, I waited at the front door of my inn for the van to arrive. As we stopped at various other hotels on the island to pick up more divers, I noticed that each person who climbed into the vehicle was hauling complicated-looking dive computers, regulators, and buoyancy-control devices. Clearly, they'd been diving for years. Me, I'd climbed aboard with my snorkel, mask, and a couple of fins.

Less than ninety minutes later, we were all sitting on a sleek dive boat in the middle of the Caribbean Sea, them in their glistening equipment, me in the additional battered gear I'd just rented from the dive operator. As we bobbed in the ocean, the dive master, an American named Mo, took out a large whiteboard and was now describing what we were about to experience.

"Okay, friends, today we're going to do a wall dive. We're going to descend right here," he said, drawing an X on the crude map he'd sketched on the whiteboard. "We'll drop to about one hundred feet. From there, we're going to swim along here"—more drawing—"before we arrive at the drop-off. This location represents the deepest point in the Caribbean Sea, about 25,000 feet below the surface."

I'm sorry, what now?

"So if there aren't any questions, let's get in the water! Don't forget to keep an eye out for your dive buddy."

One by one, the other divers made their way to the platform at the back of the boat, and with giant steps, entered the water. I shuffled my finned feet over to Mo.

"I feel like I need to let you know that I'm a really new diver, and I've only done a few dives. Also, I've never dived to one hundred feet before."

Mo frowned. "How deep have you been?"

"Um . . . maybe sixty feet?"

A flash of concern crossed his face before he grinned, perhaps a bit too widely. "You'll be fine," he said. "One hundred feet doesn't feel much different from sixty feet. Just stay close to me, and you'll be all right."

I was skeptical, but he strained to smile even wider as he nodded toward the platform. Resigned, I put the rented regulator in my mouth and made my way to where he was indicating. With one hand on my mask and regulator and the other on my weight belt, I took a deep breath and stepped off into the ocean.

The water was calm and crystal clear, the best diving conditions I'd ever experienced. Far below, I could see the other divers on the sandy bottom, bubbles from their regulators floating toward me. There was a huge splash, and Mo swam over.

"Are you okay?" he asked, using diver sign language.

"I'm okay," I signaled back. "Let's go."

Releasing air from my buoyancy-control device, I started sinking. In past dives, I'd had problems descending—the change in pressure can cause earaches—but this time I dropped easily, and soon enough, my fins were touching the sand. I checked my depth: 102 feet. I looked up at the shafts of light penetrating the water's surface above. The dive master was right: It really didn't feel any different from being at sixty feet.

Mo caught the group's attention. "Follow me," he motioned. Obediently, we began swimming. I positioned myself as close to Mo as possible.

Not a lot to see here, I thought, as we passed over a few rocks and one lazy silver fish swam by. I concentrated on slowing my breath. I may not have been an experienced diver, but I knew that slowing my breath not only had the effect of calming my nerves, but also helped conserve the precious air in my tank. I relaxed a bit, watching the rocks become larger as we swam along. Soon there were boulders all around us, and we were swimming in a narrow channel.

Suddenly, I felt a current push me forward. *What the—*

And then? *The sea bottom fell away*. The sandy floor was simply *gone*. Instead, there was nothing but blue, getting darker and darker until it was pitch black. I turned around to see where I'd come from and was stunned to be face-to-face with a giant cliff, plummeting to the inky depths. I was hovering over a chasm.

The drop-off.

I was *flying*.

Mo suddenly appeared. "Are you okay?" he signed.

I motioned back wildly. "I am *so okay!*" I yelled, sending a stream of bubbles to the surface.

I was more than okay. I was *euphoric*.

The underwater canyon was spectacular. I remained suspended, trying to find the ocean bottom and failing. The other divers were similarly entranced: We all kept looking up at the surface over one hundred feet above us, and then into the depths tens of thousands of feet below, and back again. Our collective disbelief was palpable. We were so tiny, and the ocean felt so vast. I imagined myself a speck in the ocean, and then, zooming out, the ocean being just a part of a small planet among trillions of planets in an infinite universe. The image made the conflicts of the world, not to mention my personal little life concerns, seem petty. Instead, I felt kinship—with my fellow divers, with nature, with the rest of humanity.

I felt *awe*.

Because we were so deep, we could only remain over the trench for a few minutes before methodically making our way back to the surface. I've only done a handful of dives since that day and have never again been that deep. (And for the record, I remain nervous every time I descend; I'll never be an expert diver.) But each time I return to the ocean, even for a shallow dive, I feel something of that same awe I felt over the Cayman Trench.

And it's a feeling that, honestly, I don't get enough of.

Here's the thing about awe: It feels rare and mysterious and somewhat inaccessible. If you were to ask someone—anyone—to consider the last time they felt awe, chances are they'd come up with something majestic, like looking into the Grand Canyon, or visiting the Great Wall of China. They might remember witnessing someone do something that seemed to transcend what's humanly possible, like Simone Biles landing a Yurchenko double pike vault or Jimi Hendrix wailing on his guitar. They might even mention an epic dive trip. But these instances of awe aren't exactly everyday occurrences, not to mention that some of them require substantial resources. Surely awe isn't meant only for those who have considerable downtime and financial means.

Happily, research suggests that awe is easier to access than we think. Dr. Dacher Keltner is a professor of psychology at the University of California, Berkeley, and the director of the Greater Good Science Center. He also happens to be one of the world's foremost emotion scientists. His book *Awe: The New Science of Everyday Wonder and How It Can Transform Your Life* is a radical investigation into the emotion of awe. And he maintains that we can easily cultivate awe in our daily lives.

Dr. Keltner defines awe as "the feeling of being in the presence of something vast that transcends your current understanding of the world," and he asserts that we tend to find awe when we experience what he calls the Eight Wonders of Life. The first Wonder of Life is what he describes as *moral beauty*, visible when we perceive someone exhibiting courage, kindness, strength, or resilience. Second, we experience awe in moments of *collective effervescence*; it's present, for example, when we're in a crowd that acts as a collective: spectators at a huge sporting event, or participants in a Pride march. The third Wonder of Life that inspires awe is—no surprise—*nature* (hence my overwhelm during my Cayman dive). We feel awe when we experience *beautiful, moving music* or *stirring art*. There is *spiritual* or *religious* awe, like when someone describes being in the presence of God or experiencing a transcendent meditative state. There is awe that arises from witnessing or hearing stories of *the beginning or end of life*. And the final Wonder of Life occurs during *epiphanies*: when we suddenly gain an understanding of an essential truth.

The variety of experience built into these eight wonders means that it is possible for awe to be within our reach at any moment. Not every experience of awe need be the result of a grand, overarching event—and thank heavens for that, because experiencing awe is good for us. Dr. Keltner maintains that awe changes us by quieting our overly critical egos, inspiring us to see deep patterns in life, and opening ourselves to wonder. He writes, "people who feel even five minutes a day of everyday awe are more curious about art, music, poetry, new scientific discoveries, philosophy, and questions about life and death. They feel more comfortable with mysteries, with that which cannot be explained."

Sounds like a sublime way to live. Would it, then, be possible to use intentional amateurism as a vehicle for getting to everyday awe?

My friend Steve Bennett thinks so. And he does it simply by taking care of his garden.

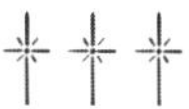

Steve is an accomplished public relations specialist and cofounder of Uncommon Caribbean, an online destination helping people reimagine Caribbean travel. Together with his brother Patrick, Steve travels around the Caribbean region, exploring and amplifying the places and stories that are often overlooked in traditional media coverage of the islands. But when Steve isn't working, you'll find him tending his lush garden behind his South Florida home.

Steve grew up on the island of Saint Croix, where his family always had a garden. "My mother was very knowledgeable about the right herbs to make bush tea," he told me. He was referring to the teas made in the Caribbean from local plants and flowers, often for medicinal purposes. "And my parents were always growing food, like papayas and bananas." Although he wasn't particularly involved in gardening when he was growing up, all that changed when he moved to New York City.

"Like a lot of island people, when I moved up north and winter came, I started to appreciate what I'd left behind," he said. "I needed to have some green around me. I had a coworker—funny enough, her name was Arhlene Flowers—and she always had potted plants in her office. She taught me how to pot my first plant."

Steve was hooked, and he began gardening in earnest. After he married, he and his wife, Kelly, moved to Florida. "We wanted a house with a garden, and when we bought our house—we still live here—the yard was a *disaster*. You could tell it had been neglected for a long time. But I was so excited. All I saw was potential."

Decades later, Steve's garden is a lush oasis, with tropical fruit trees, flowers, and wildlife. And he created it all on his own. I asked him what gardening brings to his life, and he was quiet for a moment.

"You know," he began, "it's part of my job to travel all over the Caribbean, and often when I do, I go hiking." One hike that he did on Buck Island, just off the coast of Saint Croix, has stayed with him. "I was coming down the back side of a hill, and I stopped and became very still. There was a cool breeze coming through on this very hot day. I just stood there for a moment, just to feel oneness with that space, just taking it in with all of my senses. It felt sacred."

Now, in his own garden, Steve tries to replicate a bit of that feeling. "I have a quiet area where I built a fire pit at the end of the garden. I also placed a marker there: It was the initial marker for the place where my mom is buried in Saint Croix, and I brought it back with me. I like to sit there, sipping my coffee or tea or rum, or even water. It's just a place where I can settle, and it's immensely peaceful. And on the occasions where there are butterflies or birds or dragonflies around at the same time, it's even better."

This is a beautiful example of everyday awe. But there's more: Steve shared another story with me about a time when he was able to create a moment of wonder in his garden. "At the beginning of the COVID pandemic lockdown, everybody was looking for new hobbies and things to do," he began. "And I was no different. I grew up on an island with tons of hummingbirds, and it dawned on me that I'd never seen a single hummingbird at my home, despite having lots of flowers in my yard. So I set about trying to figure out how to lure them to my garden."

Steve did a ton of research on his own, and then visited a nursery, where a staff member taught him how to mix the proper solution for hummingbird feeders and which flowers he needed to plant in his garden to attract them. He bought the plants on the spot and planted them all over the yard. He hung the feeders. And then he waited.

"At first nothing happened," he told me. "But the second year, I came out the back door to take out the trash, and there was a hummingbird hovering at the feeder close by. I just stopped in my tracks, and thought, *my God, it's working*. It fed for a few seconds and then zipped off. I was so super excited that I ran to tell Kelly. I'd worked so hard to bring them to my garden, the accomplishment felt like I'd just summitted a mountain."

The following year, there were more hummingbirds, and Steve expected that in the coming season, there would be even more. "Nowadays, I'll come out for breakfast, and they'll be feeding about an arm's length away from me. Or sometimes I come outside with my coffee, and they'll be zipping around my yard. Having them in my garden is such a callback to my childhood in St. Croix. I feel like I'm communing with them, in a way that is immensely gratifying."

Steve's avocation of tending a garden—now leveled up by creating a hummingbird habitat—has brought him beautiful, intimate moments of genuine awe.

As part of my intentional amateurism experiment, I wondered if there was something I could dabble in that might inspire similar feelings of awe. I'm not much of a gardener, nor do I have any interest in learning. And getting to the Cayman Trench again is an expensive, involved affair. Was there something I could try, something awesome, that might be a bit more accessible?

Turns out there was.

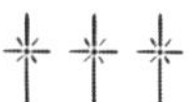

Marcus and I have had an ongoing debate for almost the entirety of our marriage. An avid camper, Marcus has slept under the stars everywhere from the moors of England to the deserts of Morocco. He insists that in those places, on very dark, cloudless nights, you can clearly see the Milky Way in all its sparkly, galactic glory.

I, on the other hand, am sane. My parents sent me to college to ensure that I would never have to sleep on the ground, so I regard camping as deeply disrespectful to their dreams for me. I refuse to do so. That said, I've certainly been outside on starry nights, sometimes in very dark places, and I flat-out do not believe it is possible to view the Milky Way without the aid of a strong telescope.

Did I mention that this argument has been going on for *years*?

Nonetheless, a secret part of me has always hoped that Marcus was right and I was wrong. So when I was booked to lead a workshop on a ranch just outside of Santa Fe, New Mexico, I wondered: Would four days in the middle of the desert with minimal light pollution make it possible to spot the Milky Way? Perhaps even *photograph* it?

A quick Google search confirmed that time of year was peak "Milky Way season" (there's a *season?*), so it was settled. Time to break out the camera equipment.

To be clear: I had no real clue how to go about doing this. Sure, I've been a photographer for decades, so I had full confidence in my ability to take portraits. I even had a few travel and photojournalistic shots in my portfolio that I was proud of. But all the images I'd ever made had been taken with the benefit of broad daylight or artful lighting. Photography, after all, means "drawing with light"; how in God's name do you shoot in *darkness*? How do you focus on something millions of miles away? Was astrophotography something you could just pick up? I was skeptical, but I packed my camera, tripod, and a couple of lenses, just in case.

The day of my trip arrived, and I landed in Albuquerque. My ride was waiting for me in baggage claim to take me out to the ranch. The cityscape quickly fell away, replaced by wild landscape: scrubby desert, cacti, and jagged, rust-colored mountains. When we eventually turned onto the main drive to the ranch an hour later, there was still five minutes of windy, dirt road that took us deeper into the desert before we arrived at the facility. There were no other neighboring properties—and therefore no distracting light sources—for miles. *Perfect*, I thought. *I'll totally be able to do this.*

The first night at the ranch was all about meeting the attendees, hosts, and other staff. The buildings were, in essence, a small boutique hotel, so our group had taken over the property. We quickly bonded over a family-style meal, cooked to perfection. This was going to be a joyful few days, to be sure. After dinner, I returned to my room, intending to turn in for the evening. But then I remembered my tripod. *I should probably try tonight*, I thought. *That way I can just get better and better each night that I'm here.* So instead of putting on pajamas, I unpacked my camera, attached my wide-angle lens, and grabbed my tripod and phone. I walked out the door and wandered away from the building, trying to get to the darkest part of the grounds.

It was only after it was dark enough that I couldn't see the path in front of me that I remembered: Deserts are teeming with snakes, scorpions, and spiders. I almost dropped my camera as I wildly fumbled for the flashlight on my phone.

Now, thoroughly nervous, I tiptoed my way to the jetty of a little pond, jumping at every faint noise along the way. I scoured the jetty with the dim light of my phone, and once I'd satisfied myself that nothing was going to eat me, I looked up. Nothing. But I'd downloaded an app on my cell phone that indicated where various constellations and the Milky Way would be at any given moment, so I found it, and pointed my phone toward the sky.

The Milky Way was apparently right over my head, and according to the app, glistening in silver and gold majesty. I lowered my camera. There was no glistening. It was a clear night, so I squinted, trying to see if I could make it out. After a while, my eyes adjusted to the darkness, and I was surprised to see the hazy outline of what had to be the Milky Way: a dim cloud of fuzzy stars, arcing right over my head. It wasn't sparkling, and it wasn't particularly majestic, but it was definitely . . . *interesting*.

My eyes might not have been able to see it clearly, but perhaps my camera could? I decided to set up my tripod and give it a go.

Have you ever tried to set up a tripod in the dark? It's damned near impossible. I could barely see my hands in front of me, so extending the legs and clicking them into place was comical, to say the least. Once I got the camera clipped into the tripod, the whole contraption kept drooping to one side. Every time I tried to shine my iPhone flashlight onto the camera to make necessary adjustments, I didn't have enough hands available to turn the dials. Finally frustrated, I just took the camera off the tripod and aimed at the sky. I fired a few shots, and then looked at the screen.

Predictably, I'd captured nothing but inky black. I sighed. *No worries*, I thought. *I've got a few more nights here. I'll just keep trying.*

And then for the next three nights, it stormed.

I'm not going to lie: I was pissed. It was in the desert—what was happening? Doesn't the word *desert* literally mean "place where it doesn't rain"? Why, then, was it actually *soggy*?

So I gave up trying to photograph the Milky Way and instead focused on my workshop. Over the course of the next few days, I mentioned that I'd hoped to photograph the galaxy to some of the attendees and, bless them, they became invested in helping me achieve this silly goal. "Oooh, it looks like it'll rain this evening," they would say, staring at their phones. "But it should clear up after two a.m." They'd look at me hopefully, heads cocked. "So . . . maybe . . . ?"

The last night, after our dinner, folks gathered around the ranch fire pit to spend a final cozy night connecting with each other. I contemplated joining them, but I also knew that I had a lot of packing to do before my driver arrived in the early morning to return me to the Albuquerque airport. As I vacillated between remaining with the group or returning to my room, it dawned on me: It had stopped raining. Tonight was my last chance.

I went back to my room and found my tripod and camera, but this time, I adjusted the settings *before* I went outside. Aperture: wide open. ISO: high. Focal length: infinite. Shutter speed: s l o w. And with my iPhone and stargazing app, I headed outside.

As I walked toward the jetty, I realized that I was calmer than the first night. Since I hadn't seen any scary animals over the previous four days, including on a short hike we'd all taken up a hill on the ranch property, I (irrationally?) believed that any snakes, scorpions, and spiders had decided to leave me alone. Instead, I listened to the sound of the buzzing cicadas, the singing crickets, and even marveled at the bats as they swooped and darted, having their evening meal of mosquitoes and other flying insects.

It was peaceful.

Suddenly, I heard my name: "*Karen!*" It was Marly, one of the guests with whom I'd spent the last few days. Marly was funny and bold and kind, and I'd liked her immediately. "Are you trying to shoot the Milky Way now?"

"Yes!" I called back. "Want to help?"

She ran toward me. When she arrived, she said, "Okay, put me to work. What do you need me to do?"

I put Marly in charge of the cell phone flashlight, as I moved the tripod legs into place. Then I showed her the star-gazing app, indicating how the Milky Was arcing over our heads, just as it had a few nights before.

"Whoa." She exhaled audibly. "That band of stars is right above us?" she asked, staring at the screen.

"Mmhmm." I turned off my phone, and we both peered into the darkness.

"I think I see it!" she said. "Is it that hazy, cloud-looking thing?"

"I think it is," I answered, nodding. "Okay, let's go."

Even though we were some distance from the brightly lit ranch, there were a couple of landscaping lights nearby. I aimed my camera at the sky just above the horizon, which my app indicated as the location of the brightest part of the Milky Way. "These ground lights are probably going to affect the shot," I said, furrowing my brow.

"I'm on it," said Marly, immediately taking off her motorcycle jacket and draping it over the nearest light. The light dimmed, and the darkness around us increased dramatically.

"Okay, here goes . . . " I pressed the button. I'd set the camera's timer so as to minimize any shake I might cause in handling the camera before the shutter opened. Marly and I stood back and waited for the telltale click.

Once the shutter opened and closed, I turned on the screen at the back of the camera. An image appeared: scrubby trees in the foreground, a misty blue background, and unmistakable stars.

"I think I got it!" I said excitedly. "Let's try again!"

For the next half hour, Marly and I took photos: I adjusted settings, and when my camera suddenly seemed to stop working, Marly coaxed it into functioning again. Cooing at and cajoling the camera, she pressed the button herself. (The camera cooperated more with her than with me, prompting her to comment, "Your camera clearly prefers my Boricua hands." I couldn't disagree.) The camera screen was too small to tell if I'd managed to get the shots I wanted, but in the moment, it didn't matter. The air was cool, nature was buzzing around us, the stars were sparkling in the sky, and I was sharing a laugh with a new friend. In the moment, all felt right with the world.

It was *awe*some.

Once I returned home and uploaded the images to my computer, I could finally see what I'd captured. The blue mistiness in the background were clouds—*damn it.* But . . . but! . . . there, peeking from behind the clouds—just a tiny bit—was the Milky Way. It wasn't the bright gold and silvery image of my phone app—not even close. But it *was* glistening, almost as if someone had dropped a small container of light blue glitter and dusted it over one tiny section of the sky. Some of the sparkles were pinpoints, but others were clustered together, shining brighter than their neighbors.

As I stared at the image on my screen, I realized I was holding my breath: I couldn't believe that I'd *almost, not quite, kind of* photographed it. I was thrilled. And I realized that I was experiencing the same emotion I'd felt hovering over the Cayman Trench: I was struck by how small I was, sitting in my little home office on this tiny rock hurtling through space in a giant, glittery galaxy. How wonderful it is to be part of this beautiful universe. How lucky we are to be here.

Even though they weren't the dream images I'd hoped to get, they were confirmation that on a clear, dark night, it's possible my camera could capture the Milky Way in its galactic glory. And despite the fact that I hadn't been fully successful in my quest, there was no question that I was sitting in my office, awash in awe. But the truth was that simply the experience of being outside, contemplating the Milky Way, was also enough to experience awe. "In fact, it is hard to imagine a single thing you can do that is better for your body and mind than finding awe outdoors," writes Keltner, who also notes that the patterns of the stars in the night sky were an inspiration for Greek, Roman, and Mesoamerican imaginings of the gods. And I must admit that even in my amateur night gazing, I couldn't help but wonder that I was looking at the same stars that astronomers have studied and ancient mariners have been using to navigate for centuries. All beings have been staring at the stars since time began. It's hard not to feel a kinship with them just by looking up at the night sky.

I haven't yet taken that elusive Milky Way photograph. Maybe next time, I'll head to Zion National Park. I hear the nights are beautifully dark for capturing the Milky Way. Maybe I'll even see it with the naked eye.

But until then, in the Great Marriage Milky Way Debate: I'm still right.

dabbling
just might be the key to
transcendence.

10 The Path to Transcendence

IT WAS 2006 in New York City, and an English teacher at Xavier High School, Ms. Lockwood, gave her students an unusual assignment: Write to a famous author and invite them to visit the school. Five of the students chose the same author, while the others chose various other authors of note. No one accepted the students' invitations to visit the school. But one—the one who received the five letters—wrote back.

Kurt Vonnegut. Here's what he said:

> I thank you for your friendly letters. You sure know how to cheer up a really old geezer (84) in his sunset years. I don't make public appearances any more because I now resemble nothing so much as an iguana.
>
> What I had to say to you, moreover, would not take long, to wit: Practice any art, music, singing, dancing, acting, drawing, painting, sculpting, poetry, fiction, essays, reportage, no matter how well or how badly, not to get money and fame, but to experience *becoming*, to find out what's inside you, *to make your soul grow*.

Seriously! I mean starting right now, do art and do it for the rest of your lives. Draw a funny or nice picture of Ms. Lockwood, and give it to her. Dance home after school, and sing in the shower and on and on. Make a face in your mashed potatoes. Pretend you're Count Dracula.

Here's an assignment for tonight, and I hope Ms. Lockwood will flunk you if you don't do it: Write a six line poem, about anything, but *rhymed*. No fair tennis without a net. Make it as good as you possibly can. But don't tell anybody what you're doing. Don't show it or recite it to anybody, not even your girlfriend or parents or whatever, or Ms. Lockwood. OK?

Tear it up into teeny-weeny pieces, and discard them into widely separated trash recepticals [*sic*]. You will find that you have already been gloriously rewarded for your poem. You have experienced becoming, learned a lot more about what's inside you, and you have made your soul grow.

God bless you all!
Kurt Vonnegut

This letter, written a mere six months before Vonnegut's death, is more than just a whimsical note intended to delight a few high school students. I think Vonnegut was letting these young people in on one of the most profound secrets of life:

that the practice of any art—indeed, any intentional habit of doing an activity for no other reason than the love of it—is the key to living a soul-filling life. His invitation to dabble in rhyming poetry isn't an argument for the students to become poets; rather, it's simply to illustrate how a single, simple act that requires some mindfulness—perhaps also a little discomfort, definitely also a little fun—can imbue the students with the sensation of *becoming*. Imagine, he implies, what would happen if you made an intentional practice of amateurism?

Make your soul grow: I think Vonnegut is onto something.

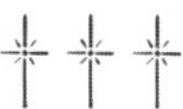

In his book *Transcend: The New Science of Self-Actualization*, psychologist and author Dr. Scott Barry Kaufman explores the theories of Abraham Maslow—he of "hierarchy of needs" fame. The traditional thinking around Maslow's hierarchy of needs is that it should be visualized as a five-tiered pyramid, with survival needs (like food, shelter, health, and connection) at the base of the pyramid, and more creative, intellectually oriented needs (like achievement, respect of others, meaning, and purpose) at the upper half of the pyramid. At the very top of the pyramid of Maslow's hierarchy is *self-actualization*, referring to the need for personal growth and discovery that is present throughout a person's life. Self-actualized people are those who are fulfilled, doing all they are capable of doing.

Dr. Kaufman, however, explodes and expands Maslow's theories, based on his research into Maslow's previously unpublished journals, lectures, essays, and other works he was unable to complete prior to his death in 1970. In doing so, Dr. Kaufman brings to light Maslow's unfinished theory of *transcendence*. First, Kaufman sets straight some of the myths surrounding Maslow's work: He asserts that viewing the hierarchy of needs as a pyramid is misinformed. The reason? The allegory of the pyramid was never created by Maslow in the first place. "[Researcher] Todd Bridgman and his colleagues examined in detail how the pyramid came to be," writes Kaufman. "[They] concluded that Maslow's pyramid was actually created by a management consultant in the sixties. From there, it quickly became popular in the emerging field or organization behavior."

Dr. Kaufman posits that a better analogy to describe the interrelationship among Maslow's needs would be that of Russian nesting dolls. Our survival needs, like connection and safety, don't vanish when we work on our intellectually-oriented needs. Instead, much like each Russian doll nests wholly in the next larger one, those needs become *integrated* into our meaning and purpose. Moreover, Dr. Kaufman reveals that at the time of his death, Maslow was working on a new theory—effectively the largest nesting doll—*the need for transcendence*. Maslow viewed transcendence as going beyond the individual growth indicated in self-actualization, even beyond health and happiness. Transcendence allows for sensing the highest levels of unity and harmony within ourselves and the world. Dr. Kaufman writes: "Transcendence is a perspective in which we can view our whole being from a higher vantage point with acceptance, wisdom and a sense of the connectedness with the rest of humanity."

In other words, transcendence is the evolution from our individual bests to our *collective* bests. It's about moving from our autonomous physiological and spiritual health to the health of the human collective. "Healthy transcendence is an emergent phenomenon resulting from the harmonious integration of one's whole self in the service of cultivating the good society," Dr. Kaufman writes. "In a nutshell: healthy transcendence involves harnessing all that you are in the service of realizing the best version of yourself, so that you can help raise the bar for the whole of humanity."

And to be clear, the "best version" of ourselves in this scenario doesn't mean wealthiest, or most prestigious, or without flaws. This isn't about perfectionism. What it *does* mean is increased mental health. A reduced fear of death. And a greater sense of purpose and altruism.

As far as how we get to self-transcendence, Maslow had an answer for this, too: He believed that the fulfillment of transcendent needs comes from *peak experiences*, which he defined as those that result in feelings of being more powerful, strengthened, and even transformed. Peak experiences are those that inspire "wonder and awe, the loss of placing in time and space . . . [and] finally, the conviction that something extremely important and valuable had happened." Dr. Kaufman expands on this, writing, "researchers define transcendent experiences as 'transient mental states marked by decreased self-salience and increased feelings of connectedness.'"

This sounds lofty, but Dr. Kaufman insists that these sorts of experiences needn't be mystical or woo-woo. "There are a variety of transcendent experiences that differ in their intensity," he maintains. Experiences range from "becoming deeply absorbed in an engrossing book, sports performance, or creative activity . . . feeling gratitude for a selfless act of kindness . . . experiencing awe at a beautiful sunset or the stars above . . . all the way up to great mystical illumination."

And most importantly, transcendence isn't about a one-and-done destination; it's about seeking out these transcendence experiences to aid in your process of *becoming*. "The good life is not something you will ever achieve. It's a way of living," says Dr. Kaufman. Transcendence, he says, is not a level, but rather "it is a north star for all humanity."

And this is where intentional amateurism comes in.

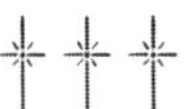

When I first embarked on this eighteen-month experiment of intentional amateurism, I thought it would be a bit of a lark: an opportunity to dabble in a few things and have some fun before moving on to my next project. As time passed, however, and as I reflected on all the conversations I'd had and research I'd done, I realized that dabbling is more than just idle amusement or merely a way to become more interesting.

Dabbling is how we find the avocation that we're going to pursue as an integral part of our self-care. It's what leads us to our intentional amateurism practice. And *that* is where the magic is.

For one thing, several people I interviewed insisted that intentional amateurism forces you to confront your own relationship to capitalism. In fact, three of them—Alice Bradley, my watercolor artist friend, automata creator Marsha Shandur, and play coach Jeff Harry—each expressed this thought, albeit more colorfully. To a person, they told me in separate conversations: "It's a giant fuck-you to capitalism!" I couldn't agree more.

Their salty and unanimous enthusiasm speaks to something profound: Hustle culture, and its attendant perfectionism and need to be productive at all costs, seeps into every aspect of our lives. Naturally, this wears us down. Our sanity exhorts us to unplug from these societal stressors, focusing, instead, on activities that bring us joy, without any concern for mastery, productivity, or financial gain. Doing so forces us to focus inward, and we thereby become more empathic and more detached from the capitalist machine.

And there's more.

Becoming an intentional amateur can help us uncover gifts we never knew we had. I'll admit it: Months later, I still can't throw a symmetrical pot on a pottery wheel to save my life. But I can get to my feet on a surfboard, an accomplishment I never would've dreamed possible.

And those wonky pots? Given that ashtrays (expert or not) just aren't that common anymore, my curiosity led me to try my hand at making scented candles. It turns out that when you fill a wonky pot with candle wax, it ceases to be a weird-looking bowl and becomes something more interesting. My candles look nothing like Mr. Budhlall's perfect diyas from the little village of my homeland. But I think of him every time I light one, and hopefully the people I give them away to enjoy them as well. A lot of love goes into each of them.

But perhaps my biggest learning is how simply embarking on an avocation with intentional amateurism is an act of mindfulness. This was true for me regardless of which attribute of intentional amateurism I'd initially set out to explore. While I discovered that many of the activities that we choose to practice as amateurs often involve more than one of the Seven Attributes, almost all of them—especially when we're just starting out—require mindfulness.

I found this particularly striking when an activity involves a repetitive element: the back and forth of a swim practice, sure, but also the spinning whir of a pottery wheel. The practice of piano scales. Knitting, running, bowling, Hula-Hooping, hair braiding: All these activities have the capacity to lull us into peaceful, meditative states. When we love doing them, they inspire a flow state, in which we can lose sense of time. Doing any of them is an act of healthy self-love, a form of spiritual care.

Similarly, mindfulness can emerge from the curiosity we feel as we examine our reactions during the exercise of our avocations. And when we dabble in various activities—whether they're brand new to us or a return to something we enjoyed in our childhood—intentional amateurism is an invitation to *awareness.* We notice our frustration with the challenges of learning (or relearning) a skill. We notice the flash of triumph when our efforts reward us. This noticing is also mindful self-care. As we notice our reactions and practice self-compassion in response, we acknowledge our common humanity. Our successes and failures as we proceed in the practice of the things we love remind us of the experiences in life that we *all* face. These peaks and valleys are part of our common human experience around the world.

Moreover, the discovery of our ability to stretch our comfort zones—and the attendant euphoria when we do—can evoke feelings of awe. Who knew we were capable of *surfing?* Skydiving? Making a soufflé? Even better: When we're able to do these activities alongside those with whom we feel a connection, or even in collective effervescence—well, the awe we experience is magnified.

In the interest of full transparency, I must admit that not every activity I dabbled in will be a part of my intentional amateurism going forward. I *loved* surfing, but my proximity to a surfable beach—or lack thereof—makes it impossible for me to practice it with a meaningful cadence going forward. Similarly, as much as Marcus and I enjoyed sailing, it's a bit of a trek for us to get to a marina. But despite similar challenges in accessing dark skies, I'm determined to photograph that Milky Way as often as opportunity allows. Also, I now have a membership to a pottery studio, and I make an effort to find myself in front of a wheel a few times every month. I even love spending time on my piano keyboard each week. And most surprisingly, I'm still a regular at our local pool, chlorine and all. Because I dabbled, I have become a total amateur at a few new activities that I truly enjoy, ones that allow me to practice all Seven Attributes of Intentional Amateurism.

And the best part? My practice of intentional amateurism has invited more serendipity, gratitude, and joy into my life. By mindfully doing something I love, whether it's pottery or piano, I automatically have something to be grateful for at the end of the day. And perhaps this is a new definition of success: not financial wealth or technical superiority, but instead, the ability to create moments of joy, to connect with those who have similar interests, and to tap into self-compassion, mindfulness, and just plain fun, *at will.* With intentional amateurism, we create opportunities for which to be grateful. Over time, those experiences can add up to an indisputably joyful life. Let me repeat: Practicing intentional amateurism allows us to take control of bringing more joy into our lives. Can you imagine?

Dr. Kaufman tells us that all these things—beauty, connection, exploration, love, flow, creativity, purpose and even gratitude—are transcendent experiences. The beauty of the

Seven Attributes of Intentional Amateurism is that they provide the scaffolding and the mindset that helps us access these transcendent experiences more readily. This, ultimately, is why a practice of intentional amateurism is essential: I believe it should be a fundamental in our life approach. Intentional amateurism increases our opportunity for peak experiences and in so doing, helps move us in the direction of the most exalted of Maslow's needs.

But there's an outstanding elephant-in-the-room question that remains. Is transcendence actually a *need*, or is it something that would just be nice to have?

This question is central to the humanist school of psychology. Launched by Maslow in 1961, the humanist psychology framework defines a healthy personality as one that moves toward freedom, responsibility, self-awareness, and personal growth, rather than status, achievement, and success. Building on this, in the 1990s psychologist Dr. Martin Seligman evolved humanist psychology by galvanizing the field of *positive psychology*, generating even more rigorous scientific research on well-being.

Make no mistake: This was a revolution. Rather than the traditional psychological focus of defining and diagnosing disease, disorder, and dysfunction, both humanist and positive psychology examine what it takes for a person to thrive. Diagnosis is important, of course, but can only take us so far in living a fulfilled life. Positive psychology researcher Shawn Achor puts it this way: "You can eliminate depression without making someone happy. You can cure anxiety without teaching someone optimism. You can return someone to work without improving their job performance. If all you strive for is diminishing the bad, you'll only attain the average, and you'll miss out entirely on the opportunity to exceed the average. You can study gravity forever without learning how to fly."

So asking the question again: Is transcendence—or really, any of the intellectually oriented needs theorized by Maslow—actually necessary? Perhaps not for survival, no. But for thriving? *Absolutely*. And by simply creating a practice of doing what we love, we create opportunities for transcendence to occur. We enjoy the practice in the moment, but we also enjoy the benefits of the practice in our everyday lives.

Like Camille, for example, my friend who walked the South West Coast Path with her friend Lindsey: She tells how the two-month adventure changed them both. "There was something about connecting with each other that helped each of us connect with ourselves," she told me. "I know that for me, I've always struggled with belonging, but since that trek, I'm clearer about belonging to the wide world, belonging to *myself*. And I've even noticed a shift in Lindsey. She seems braver since our trek, and she's exploring new things. Doing this walk, perhaps *especially* because we weren't hikers before, showed us how our identities could change. We could detach from self-perceptions, or the perceptions other people have of who we are, all just by doing a new thing."

Or take Jenn Romolini, my weaving friend, who says she learns more about herself and her own motivations through her intentional amateurism practice. "For me, staying an amateur allows me to open my heart to myself. It takes the pressure of succeeding out of the question, and frankly, it pulls me out of my professional identity. And that's the other thing that's important: I think we all tend to equate happiness with success. We intertwine our identities with our profession. For me, it's important that I have an amateur practice, because that professional grind mindset can shut me down, and I don't want that. I want to be expansive."

And Marsha Shandur insists that practicing her passion as an amateur automata creator adds so much to her life: "It's honestly one of the things that gives me the most pleasure in the whole world. When I'm tinkering, I feel connected to myself and to the universe, and feel deeply at peace in a way that only being consumed by art can make me feel."

Detaching from perceptions, being expansive, feeling connected to self and universe: *This* is what it means to thrive. And with so much darkness in the world, we owe it to ourselves to create light in our lives wherever we can. So go ahead: Dabble in whittling. Take that hip-hop class. Dust off the karaoke machine. Do the thing that quietly calls to you, enticing you to try something new or to return to something old. Do it to satisfy your curiosity, play with your comfort zone's edge, connect with a loved one, or practice mindfulness. Doing so will help you discover that thing you love, that activity that fuels your self-compassion, that avocation that you love doing simply because it brings you nothing more than joy. Kurt Vonnegut says that intentionally practicing your newfound pastime will help you experience *becoming*, and he's right.

And while I don't know if intentional amateurism will actually make your soul *grow*, all evidence suggests it will make your soul shine more brilliantly than ever.

So do it.

You total amateur, you.

ABRIDGED LIST OF AMATEUR PURSUITS

THINGS I TRIED AND DIDN'T TRY (BUT STILL MIGHT)

- wheel-thrown pottery making
- swimming
- piano playing
- filmmaking
- surfing
- sailing
- astrophotography
- jazz singing
- drumming
- roller-skating
- ice-skating
- flying trapeze
- aerial silks
- sculling
- knitting
- sewing
- baking macarons
- making pasta from scratch
- French-cuisine cooking
- acrylic painting
- making mosaics
- cycling
- unicycling

steelpan playing
tap dancing
juggling
acting
improv
playing guitar
African dancing
belly dancing
writing poetry
origami
macramé
interior design
fashion design
graphic design
calligraphy
hiking
millinery
silversmithing

ballet
quilting
Asian cooking
auto mechanics
learning Spanish
learning French
learning Chinese
genealogy
hand beading
tarot-card reading
watercolor painting
hair braiding
flower arranging
windsurfing
gardening
orchid growing
bonsai-tree cultivating
bartending

shoemaking
cartooning
graffiti making
home renovation
carpentry
metalworking
bookbinding
wood carving
glassblowing
fabric weaving
harp playing
soapmaking
sculpture
DJ mixing
winemaking
coffee roasting
yoga
Pilates
block printing
tai chi
bell ringing
clockmaking
lace tatting
eggroll making
card shuffling
magic tricks
horseback riding
beekeeping
darts
archery
cross-country skiing
leatherworking
podcasting
kayaking
animation
furniture building

architectural modeling
tango dancing
salsa dancing
cumbia dancing
bachata dancing
astrology
mehndi
coffee art
basket weaving
billiards
bowling
cake decorating
carpet weaving
chocolate making
handwriting analysis
harmonica
pickling
making automata

bicycle maintenance
weightlifting
jogging
pickleball
tennis
mountain climbing
bouldering
artistic swimming
breakdancing
trainspotting
birdwatching
judo
ice hockey
fencing
water polo
snowshoeing
downhill skiing
snowboarding

skateboarding
hand-building pottery
poker playing
twerking
whittling
collage
skydiving
parasailing
paragliding
hot-air ballooning
deep-sea fishing
fly fishing
fossil hunting
Reiki
astronomy
UFO hunting
Egyptology
stamp collecting
yodeling
stilt walking
animal training
storm chasing
dressage
LEGO-brick building
silk-screening
drone flying
ham-radio operation
ghost hunting
scrapbooking
spelunking
playwriting
stand-up comedy
car racing
chain-mail crafting
skeet shooting
plane spotting

light-aircraft piloting

falconry

BASE jumping

rafting

iceboating

dogsledding

tobogganing

pole dancing

Dungeons & Dragons

computer coding

video-gaming design

upholstering

furniture renewing

house flipping

citizen journalism

geocaching

making sailing knots

beer making

dollhouse building

train-set building

robot making

coin collecting

geology

entomology

adventure travel

musical-instrument building

chicken raising

true crime investigating

modeling

birdhouse building

capoeira

Rube Goldberg-machine designing

fishing-lure making
fan-fiction writing
chess playing
wrestling
friendship-bracelet making
cosplay
thrifting
makeup artistry
flow arts
beachcombing
metal detecting
dollmaking
meat smoking
urban farming
nail art
fermenting
fire breathing
miniature building
coloring books
balloon-animal making
floral arranging
bagpiping
go-karting
RVing
slacklining
rock painting
card games
sandcastle building
kite flying
candy making
open-water swimming

ACKNOWLEDGMENTS

IN BRINGING THIS book into being, it quickly became clear that there were two distinct challenges. One, of course, was *the actual writing of the book*. But the other was *embracing being a total amateur*. Make no mistake: Being a total amateur isn't for the fainthearted; and as you embark on your intentional amateurism journey, one of the most rewarding things you can do is surround yourself with wise people who can both share their own inspiring stories with you and guide you in your own practice. You heard it here first.

To that end, my deepest gratitude to Aimee Woodall, Alice Bradley, Camille Van Hoegaerden, Denise Wade, Jenn Romolini, John Brockland, Marsha Shandur, and Steve Bennett, for generously sharing their avocations and their undeniable wisdom with me. This book could not have been written without you, and the world is a better place for your joyful dabbling. Thank you.

Thanks also to the people who helped guide me in my dabbling quests: first, to Bea Arman Fiorito and Heather Gritz of HTX Clay, for your patience in teaching me the ways of the wheel. Because of you, I was able to transform my work from expert ashtrays to interesting pet bowls to, finally, ~~wonky~~ charming candles, and that is far more than I ever expected to do. (One day I'll pull the walls high enough to make an actual vase. *One day.*) I'm also grateful to South Coast Sailing Adventures for awakening dreams of tacking across the wind on crystalline seas—we'll be back. Thanks also to Francisco and Josue of Line Up Surf School in Los Cabos, Mexico, for their apparently limitless patience, and for also making sure we didn't scrape our faces on the rocks on the beach. I hope we can visit again! And finally, to Marly Rivera, my guardian angel in the desert: Thanks for joining me in my hunt for the Milky Way, for clapping to keep the bats away, and for cajoling my camera into functioning. Searching for the Milky Way was *awesome*, in the word's most traditional sense, and I'm glad I could share it with you.

And for the folks who helped me put pen to paper: My deep gratitude to Jeff Harry, Maggie Mason, Joon S. Park, and Peter Calin, for sharing their expertise in paramount play, magical life lists, and everyday mindfulness, respectively. Our conversations were critical in helping me understand the huge benefits of intentional amateurism. Thanks always to my editor, Valerie Weaver-Zercher, and her magical gift for taking my words and making them shine. To my friends, A'Driane Nieves, Asha Dornfest, Laura Mayes, Mark Savage, and Sarayu Blue, who were always there with texts, voicemails, and other words of encouragement, including, but not limited to: "I'll give you some advice I learned in college: As you approach your book deadline and are feeling stressed, if you eat a huge bag of Fritos and drink a two-liter bottle of Mountain Dew, it will make you feel terrible," *Noted*, and thank you all for always making me feel like I can do this writing thing.

To my parents, Kermitt and Yvette Walrond, and to my sister, Natalie Walrond: Thanks for always being my cheerleaders. To my daughter Alexis: I love you so much, and you make me so proud. Thanks for always making me laugh and laugh.

And to my Marcus: Thank you for always being up for any adventure, and for your unwavering support. You are my favorite amateur, and I love you madly.

NOTES

Chapter 1: A Case for Intentional Amateurism

3 ***word* amateur *is derived from the Latin* amare*, meaning "to love":*** *Oxford English Dictionary*, "amateur," accessed July 14, 2023, https://www.oxfordreference.com/view/10.1093/oi/authority.20110803095406990.

3 ***"was already being used in the somewhat condescending extended sense":*** *Merriam-Webster Dictionary*, "amateur," accessed August 7, 2024, https://www.merriam-webster.com/dictionary/amateur.

4 ***"striving to be extraordinary, being exceptional, and being special":*** Rainesford Stauffer, *An Ordinary Age: Finding Your Way in a World That Expects Exceptional* (HarperCollins, 2021), 2.

4 ***"the more 'free time' pursuits get crossed off the list":*** Stauffer, *Ordinary Age*, 80–81.

6 ***"Perfectionism is the belief that if we live perfect, look perfect, and act perfect":*** Brené Brown, *The Gifts of Imperfection: 10th Anniversary Edition* (Random House, 2020), 75.

6 ***"relentless pursuit of flawlessness can lead to low self-worth":*** Tracy Dennis-Tiwary, "Perfectionists: Lowering Your Standards Can Improve Your Mental Health," *The Washington Post*, October 19, 2022, https://www.washingtonpost.com/wellness/2022/10/19/perfectionism-anxiety-excellence/.

6 ***"it's the thing that's really preventing us from taking flight":*** Brown, *Gifts of Imperfection*, 75.

6 ***fewer symptoms of depression, and higher life satisfaction:*** Heidi Godman, "Having a Hobby Tied to Happiness and Well-Being," *Harvard Health Letter*, January 1, 2024, https://www.health.harvard.edu/mind-and-mood/having-a-hobby-tied-to-happiness-and-well-being.

7 ***the amateur stays in the place of the "constant now":*** Sarah Lewis, *The Rise: Creativity, the Gift of Failure, and the Search for Mastery* (Simon & Schuster, 2015), 151–52.

9 ***defined as trying an activity for a short period:*** *Cambridge Dictionary*, "dabble," accessed December 9, 2024, https://dictionary.cambridge.org/us/dictionary/english/dabble.

10 ***"make room in your life for curiosity and adventure":*** Norma Kamali, *Norma Kamali: I Am Invisible* (Abrams Books, 2021), 178.

12 ***"we're denying ourselves the thing we actually want most":*** Kristin Neff, *Self-Compassion: The Proven Power of Being Kind to Yourself* (William Morrow, 2015), 158.

14 ***stretching our comfort zones can be good for us:*** Korin Miller, "Stepping out of Your Comfort Zone Is Good for You—Here's How to Do It, According to Therapists." Well+Good, December 17, 2021, https://www.wellandgood.com/stepping-out-of-your-comfort-zone/.

15 ***calls our global grappling with perfectionism an "epidemic":*** Thomas Curran, *The Perfection Trap: Embracing the Power of Good Enough* (Scribner, 2023), 80–81.

15 ***"Social media threatens to make every slip-up an extinction-level event":*** Arthur C. Brooks, "Go Ahead and Fail," *The Atlantic*, April 7, 2022,

https://www.theatlantic.com/family/archive/2021/02/how-overcome-fear-failure/618130/.

16 ***"parts of our brains that are associated with our ego":*** Barbara Palmer, "Everyday Awe and Its Effects on Our Brains," PCMA Convene (blog), PCMA, March 31, 2023, https://www.pcma.org/everyday-awe-effects-on-our-brains/.

17 ***"If you want to change your life, change what you pay attention to":*** Austin Kleon, *Keep Going: 10 Ways to Stay Creative in Good Times and Bad* (Workman, 2019), 101.

Chapter 2: The Spirituality of Intentional Amateurism and the Making of an Amateur's Menu

21 ***"You don't have to always be creating, doing and contributing to the world":*** Tricia Hersey, *Rest Is Resistance: A Manifesto* (Little, Brown Spark, 2022), 151.

21 ***"Rest is radical because it disrupts the lie that we are not doing enough":*** Hersey, *Rest Is Resistance*, 7.

21 ***we are spiritual beings navigating a material world:*** Hersey, *Rest Is Resistance,* 17.

22 ***"the major event of my day became a trip to the shower":*** Casper ter Kuile, *The Power of Ritual: Turning Everyday Activities into Soulful Practices* (HarperOne, 2021).

22 ***"Nothing frustrates me more than failing in public":*** Ter Kuile, *Power of Ritual*, 32.

23 ***"a powerful, perhaps even spiritual way of connecting to myself":*** Ter Kuile, *Power of Ritual*, 33.

23 ***"rituals make the invisible connections that make life meaningful, visible":*** Ter Kuile, *Power of Ritual*, 26.

33 ***we are much more likely to have* boldness regret—*regret over the chances we* didn't *take:*** Daniel H. Pink, *The Power of Regret: How Looking Backward Moves Us Forward* (Riverhead Books, 2022), 78.

33 ***"a counterfactual in which we were more daring, and consequently, more fulfilled":*** Pink, *Power of Regret*, 100.

Chapter 3: Curiosity

42 ***India has a long tradition of clay pottery:*** Shastri Boodan, "Pottery Making Still Taking Shape in Trinidad," *Trinidad & Tobago Guardian*, May 5, 2012, https://www.guardian.co.tt/article-6.2.421741.db5ec1cab1.

54 ***"the person who makes something today isn't the same person who returns to the work tomorrow":*** Rick Rubin, *The Creative Act: A Way of Being* (Penguin Press, 2023), 57.

Chapter 4: Mindfulness

62 ***the "attitudes of mindfulness":*** Jon Kabat-Zinn, "The Mindful Attitude of Patience by Jon Kabat-Zinn," Mindfulness Training, Mindfulness-Based Stress Reduction, accessed May 6, 2024, https://mbsrtraining.com/attitudes-of-mindfulness-by-jon-kabat-zinn/mindful-attitude-of-patience-jon-kabat-zinn/.

63 ***"Being mindful allows us to be joyfully engaged in what we are doing":*** Ellen Langer, *Mindfulness: 25th Anniversary Edition* (Da Capo Press, 2021), 26.

63 ***"We can choose how to respond to a given event, rather than being hijacked by our emotions":*** M. J. Ryan, *The Power of Patience: How This Old-Fashioned Virtue Can Improve Your Life* (Conari Press, 2021), 21.

64 ***"If you cultivate patience, you almost can't help but cultivate mindfulness":*** Jon Kabat-Zinn, *Wherever You Go, There You Are: Mindfulness Meditation in Everyday Life* (Hachette Books 2005), 55.

66 **mindfulness *as the awareness that arises through paying attention:*** Jon Kabat-Zinn, "Me Me Me" *Mindful*, YouTube, May 28, 2015, https://www.youtube.com/watch?v=ULJSacYFzzQ.

66 ***flow refers to the experience of an activity that is so thoroughly engrossing:*** Mihaly Csikszentmihalyi, *Flow: The Psychology of Optimal Experience* (Harper Perennial Modern Classics, 2008), 62.

67 ***mindfulness and flow are similar—both emphasize the value of living in the moment:*** Hao Chen, et al., "How Flow and Mindfulness Interact with Each Other in Mindfulness-Based Augmented Reality Mandala Coloring Activities," *Frontiers in Psychology* 14 (January 2024), doi:10.3389/fpsyg.2023.1301531.

67 ***mindfulness can provide the* basis *of flow:*** "Mindfulness and Flow: Being 'in the Zone,'" Mindfulness Breathing Lab, Mayo Clinic Connect (blog), December 22, 2016, https://connect.mayoclinic.org/blog/mindfulness-in-health/newsfeed-post/5-mindfulness-and-flow/.

68 ***swimming practice reminded him of when he was first learning the basics of meditation:*** Light Watkins, "Debunking the 5 Most Common Meditation Myths," TEDTalk, Venice, CA, February 22, 2015, transcription

published on Singju Post website, June 14, 2020, https://singjupost.com/light-watkins-debunking-5-common-meditation-myths-transcript/.

Chapter 5: Self-Compassion

79 ***By high school, he was playing in piano bars to help his family make ends meet:*** "Billy Joel," 2013 Kennedy Center Honoree introduction, official website of The Kennedy Center, https://www.kennedy-center.org/artists/j/jo-jz/billy-joel/.

79 ***"If I'm not going to Columbia University, I'm going to Columbia Records":*** "Billy Joel," Wikipedia, accessed July 20, 2024, https://en.wikipedia.org/wiki/Billy_Joel.

79 ***"Piano Man"—the title track of Joel's debut album—was his first Top 20 single:*** "Billy Joel," https://en.wikipedia.org/wiki/Billy_Joel.

79 ***His album* An Innocent Man *had six Top 40 singles:*** "Billy Joel Biography," on Billy Joel's official website, accessed January 15, 2022, https://www.billyjoel.com/biography/.

79 ***the recipient of the Grammy Legend Award and is a Kennedy Center honoree:*** "Billy Joel Biography," https://www.billyjoel.com/biography/.

80 ***"I said, 'That's my problem. I have not forgiven myself for not being Beethoven'":*** "'Piano Man' Billy Joel on Hitting the 100 Mark at Madison Square Garden," CBS Interactive, July 22, 2018, https://cbsnews.com/news/piano-man-billy-joel-on-hitting-the-100-mark-at-madison-square-garden/.

80 ***Perfectionism is the compulsive need to achieve and accomplish goals:*** Kristin Neff, *Self-Compassion: The Proven Power of Being Kind to Yourself* (William Morrow, 2015), 69.

80 ***unchecked perfectionism affects our health:*** Brian Swider, et al., "The Pros and Cons of Perfectionism, According to Research." *Harvard Business Review*, September 17, 2021, https://hbr.org/2018/12/the-pros-and-cons-of-perfectionism-according-to-research.

81 ***"Perfectionism is other-focused: what will they think?":*** Brené Brown, *Daring Greatly: How the Courage to Be Vulnerable Transforms the Way We Live, Love, Parent, and Lead* (Avery, 2015), 129.

81 ***When we practice self-compassion, we cultivate emotional resilience:*** Neff, *Self-Compassion*, 108.

81 ***maintain that sense of elevated self-esteem, they fall into traps like narcissism:*** Neff, *Self-Compassion*, 8.

82 ***"self-compassion provides the same benefits as high self-esteem":*** Neff, *Self-Compassion*, 8.

82 ***research indicates that increased levels of oxytocin amplify feelings:*** Neff, *Self-Compassion*, 47.

86 ***"acceptance of what's occurring in the present moment":*** Neff, *Self-Compassion*, 80.

87 ***recognition of our* common humanity*:*** Neff, *Self-Compassion*, 41.

87 ***final element of self-compassion is* self-kindness*:*** Neff, *Self-Compassion*, 41.

88 ***we can give ourselves "self-compassion breaks":*** Kristin Neff, "Exercise 2: Self-Compassion Break," Self-Compassion website, accessed May 4, 2024, https://self-compassion.org/exercises/exercise-2-self-compassion-break/.

Chapter 6: Play

98 ***"the sheer demands of daily living seem to rob us of the ability to play":*** Stuart L. Brown and Christopher C. Vaughn, *Play: How It Shapes the Brain, Opens the Imagination and Invigorates the Soul* (Avery, 2010), 6–7.

98 ***we end up actually shaming ourselves into giving up play:*** Brown and Vaughn, *Play*, 145.

99 ***play activity helps to sculpt the brain:*** Brown and Vaughn, *Play*, 34.

99 ***It helps make us—and our worlds—new again:*** Brown and Vaughn, *Play*, 127.

99 ***"the opposite of play is depression":*** Brown and Vaughn, *Play*, 126.

102 ***According to Dr. Stuart Brown, there are seven properties of play:*** Brown and Vaughn, *Play*, 17–18.

102 ***"When we ignore play, we start to have problems":*** Brown and Vaughn, *Play*, 201.

Chapter 7: Stretch Zone

113 **@CNNBRK: Diana Nyad about 2 miles from end of Cuba-to-Florida swim:** CNN Breaking News (@cnnbrk), "Diana Nyad about 2 miles from end of Cuba-to-Florida swim, team says," X (Formerly Twitter), September 2, 2013, x.com/cnnbrk/status/374560497816711168.

114 ***first person ever to swim across the Florida Straits:*** "Diana Nyad Arrives in Key West After 111-Mile Swim from Cuba." FloridaKeysTV, September 2, 2013, Video, 2 min., 36 sec., YouTube, https:// www.youtube.com/watch?v=mcvjiw582G0.

115 ***"risk-taking is enlivening, because it helps expand our self-definition":*** Julia Cameron, *The Artist's Way: A Spiritual Path to Higher Creativity* (Jeremy P. Tarcher/Putnam, 1996), 122.

116 ***when we step outside of our comfort zones, we become more resilient:*** Abigail Brenner, "5 Benefits of Stepping Outside Your Comfort Zone," *Psychology Today*, December 27, 2015, https://www.psychologytoday.com/us/blog/in-flux/201512/5-benefits-stepping-outside-your-comfort-zone.

116 ***Our awareness of the world expands:*** Jessica A. Kent, "Is It Time to Leave Your Comfort Zone? How Leaving Can Spark Positive Change," *Harvard Summer School* (blog), Harvard School of Continuing Education, August 28, 2023, https://summer.harvard.edu/blog/leaving-your-comfort-zone/.

116 ***Our awareness of the world expands:*** Kent, "Time to Leave."

116 ***She distinguishes it from our "complacency zone":*** Kristen Butler, *The Comfort Zone: Create a Life You Really Love with Less Stress and More Flow* (Hay House, 2023), 27.

117 ***"you listen to your own inner guidance rather than to the suggestions of others":*** Butler, *Comfort Zone*, 36.

117 ***known in the 1970s as the world's greatest long-distance swimmer:*** Diana Nyad, "Bio," Diana Nyad's official website, accessed August 12, 2024, https://diananyad.com/bio.

118 ***"I'm walking around tall because I am [a] bold, fearless person":*** Diana Nyad, "Never, Ever Give Up." TEDWomen, San Francisco, CA, December

2013, 14:40, https://www.ted.com/talks/diana_nyad_never_ever_give_up.

Chapter 8: Connection

138 ***"A human moment," he writes, "occurs any time two or more people are together":*** Edward M. Hallowell, *Connect: 12 Vital Ties That Open Your Heart, Lengthen Your Life, and Deepen Your Soul* (Pocket Books, 1999), 9.

138 ***"feeling a part of something larger than yourself":*** Hallowell, *Connect,* 22.

140 **social health *means "the aspect of overall health and well-being that comes from connection":*** Kasley Killam, *The Art and Science of Connection: Why Social Health Is the Missing Key to Living Longer, Healthier, and Happier* (HarperOne, 2024), 2.

140 ***"Loneliness ran like a dark thread through many of the more obvious issues":*** Vivek Murthy, *Together: The Healing Power of Human Connection in an Often Lonely World* (Harper Wave, 2020), xiv.

141 ***in 2023, the Office of the Surgeon General issued a health advisory:*** Vivek Murthy, "Our Epidemic of Loneliness and Isolation," The US Surgeon General's Advisory on the Healing Effects of Social Connection and Community (Washington, D.C., 2023), https://www.hhs.gov/sites/default/files/surgeon-general-social-connection-advisory.pdf.

141 ***"People with strong social relationships are fifty percent less likely to die prematurely":*** Murthy, *Together,* 13.

141 ***"it's a biological and social imperative":*** Murthy, *Together*, 29.

141 ***"Our ancestors' default setting was togetherness":*** Murthy, *Together*, 31.

141 ***"Connection is an essential vitamin":*** Hallowell, *Connect*, 12.

142 ***dedicate at least one hour each day to social interaction:*** Killam, *Art and Science*, 72.

142 ***"best ways to strengthen your social muscles":*** Killam, *Art and Science*, 118.

142 ***"the more time you spend with someone, the closer you become":*** Killam, *Art and Science*, 120.

147 ***It is the face-to-face interactions, both in the doing and the recollecting:*** Hallowell, *Connect*, 175.

148 ***an integral part of the trust-building process:*** Brené Brown, *Daring Greatly: How the Courage to Be Vulnerable Transforms the Way We Live, Love, Parent, and Lead* (Avery, 2015), 45–46.

Chapter 9: Wonder and Awe

156 ***one of the world's foremost emotion scientists:*** "Bio," on Dacher Keltner's website, accessed August 21, 2024, https://www.dacherkeltner.com/bio.

156 ***"being in the presence of something vast":*** Dacher Keltner, *Awe: The New Science of Everyday Wonder and How It Can Transform Your Life* (Penguin Press, 2023), 6.

157 ***what he calls the Eight Wonders of Life:*** Keltner, *Awe*, 10–18.

157 ***awe changes us by quieting our overly critical egos:*** Keltner, *Awe*, xx.

157 ***"They feel more comfortable with mysteries, with that which cannot be explained":*** Keltner, *Awe*, 39.

169 ***"better for your body and mind than finding awe outdoors":*** Keltner, *Awe*, 127.

169 ***an inspiration for Greek, Roman, and Mesoamerican imaginings of the gods:*** Keltner, *Awe*, 13.

Chapter 10: The Path to Transcendence

174 ***"to experience becoming, to find out what's inside you, to make your soul grow":*** Cynthia L. Haven, "Kurt Vonnegut's Advice to Students: 'Dance Home after School . . . Make a Face in Your Mashed Potatoes. Pretend You're Count Dracula,'" The Book Haven (blog), Stanford University, May 2, 2022, https://bookhaven.stanford.edu/2022/05/kurt-vonneguts-advice-to-students-dance-home-after-school-make-a-face-in-your-mashed-potatoes-pretend-youre-count-dracula/.

175 ***Maslow's hierarchy of needs:*** Saul McLeod, "Maslow's Hierarchy of Needs." *Simply Psychology*, January 24, 2024, https://www.simplypsychology.org/maslow.html#What-is-Maslows-Hierarchy-of-Needs.

175 **self-actualization,** ***referring to the need for personal growth:*** McLeod, "Maslow's Hierarchy."

176 ***Maslow's pyramid was actually created by a management consultant:*** Scott Barry Kaufman, *Transcend: The New Science of Self-Actualization* (TarcherPerigee, 2020), xxviii.

176 ***each Russian doll nests wholly in the next larger one, those needs become*** **integrated:** Kaufman, *Transcend*, xxvii.

176 ***Transcendence allows for sensing the highest levels of unity and harmony:*** Kaufman, *Transcend*, xxxiv.

177 ***"a perspective in which we can view our whole being":*** Kaufman, *Transcend*, xxxiv.

177 ***"integration of one's whole self in the service of cultivating the good society":*** Kaufman, *Transcend*, 217.

177 ***"a greater sense of purpose and altruism":*** Kaufman, *Transcend*, 203.

177 ***inspire "wonder and awe, the loss of placing in time and space":*** Matt Davis, "Maslow's Forgotten Pinnacle: Self-Transcendence," *Big Think*, April 19, 2022, https://bigthink.com/neuropsych/maslow-self-transcendence/.

178 ***""marked by decreased self-salience and increased feelings of connectedness"":*** Kaufman, *Transcend,* 202.

178 ***"transcendent experiences that differ in their intensity":*** Kaufman, *Transcend*, 201.

178 ***"It's a way of living":*** Kaufman, *Transcend*, xxxvii.

178 ***"it is a north star for all humanity":*** Kaufman, *Transcend*, 218.

182 ***and even gratitude—are transcendent experiences:*** Kaufman, *Transcend*, xx.

183 ***the humanist psychology framework defines a healthy personality as:*** Kaufman, *Transcend*, xx.

183 ***field of* positive psychology*:*** Kaufman, *Transcend*, xx.

184 ***"If all you strive for is diminishing the bad, you'll only attain the average":*** Shawn Achor, *The Happiness Advantage: How a Positive Brain Fuels Success in Work and Life* (Currency, 2018), 10.